Essentials of Transfer Pricing

Steven M. Bragg

AccountingTools®

ISBN 978-1-64221338-6

For more information about AccountingTools® products, visit our Web site at www.accountingtools.com.

Table of Contents

About the Author

Steven Bragg, CPA, has been the chief financial officer or controller of four companies, as well as a consulting manager at Ernst & Young. He received a master's degree in finance from Bentley College, an MBA from Babson College, and a Bachelor's degree in Economics from the University of Maine. He has been a two-time president of the Colorado Mountain Club, and is an avid alpine skier, mountain biker, and certified master diver. Mr. Bragg resides in Centennial, Colorado. He has written more than 300 books and courses, including *New Controller Guidebook*, *GAAP Guidebook*, and *Payroll Management*. He has also written *The Auditors* science fiction trilogy.

Steven maintains the accountingtools.com web site, which contains continuing professional education courses, the Accounting Best Practices podcast, and thousands of articles on accounting subjects.

Buy Additional AccountingTools Courses

AccountingTools offers more than 1,500 hours of CPE courses, with concentrations in accounting, auditing, finance, taxation, and ethics. Related courses that you might like include:

- CFO Guidebook
- Cost Accounting Fundamentals
- Pricing for Profit

Go to accountingtools.com/cpe to view these additional courses.

AccountingTools®

Essentials of Transfer Pricing

Introduction

Some companies have chosen to become vertically integrated, which means that one subsidiary creates a product or service that is used by another subsidiary in *its* products. When these subsidiaries are located in different tax jurisdictions, it is possible for a business to adjust the prices at which the components are shifted from one entity to another, so that the bulk of the associated profits are recognized in a low-tax jurisdiction. Recognizing this issue, governments have imposed a number of rules that mandate how transfer prices are to be calculated. In this course, we discuss the nature of transfer prices, the regulations that mandate how the prices are devised, and the several methods available for doing so. The course also addresses a number of related issues, such as comparability analysis, documentation requirements, and dispute resolution procedures.

What is Transfer Pricing?

Transfer pricing refers to the pricing of goods, services, or intangible assets exchanged between the related entities of a multinational enterprise. Because these transactions occur within the same corporate group rather than between independent parties, there is a risk that prices may be manipulated to shift profits to low-tax jurisdictions, thereby reducing the overall tax burden of the group.

To prevent such distortions, tax authorities worldwide require that transfer prices follow the arm's length principle, which states that the prices charged between related entities should be equivalent to those that would be agreed upon by independent parties under comparable circumstances. Achieving this requires careful analysis of the functions performed, assets employed, and risks assumed by each entity, along with comparisons to independent transactions (known as *comparables*).

Several methods are used to test transfer pricing compliance; the choice of method depends on the nature of the transaction, data availability, and industry practices. Ultimately, transfer pricing serves a dual purpose: ensuring the fair allocation of profits among jurisdictions and preventing tax avoidance, while also allowing businesses to structure cross-border operations in a compliant and sustainable way.

The Historical Development of Transfer Pricing Rules

The historical development of transfer pricing rules reflects a long struggle by governments to balance multinational corporate flexibility with the need to preserve national tax bases. The evolution can be traced across three main phases: early domestic measures, international standard-setting, and the modern era of global coordination and reform.

Early Domestic Measures

The earliest transfer pricing rules appeared in the United States in the 1920s, when Congress became concerned that multinational corporations could manipulate inter-company pricing to shift profits abroad and reduce U.S. taxable income. Section 45 of the Revenue Act of 1928 gave the Commissioner of Internal Revenue the authority to reallocate income among related parties to reflect an "arm's length" outcome. This established the foundational principle that transfer prices between related parties should mirror the prices charged in comparable transactions between independent parties. Other countries, including Germany and Canada, introduced similar rules during the 1930s and 1940s as they confronted tax base erosion.

International Standard-Setting

The post–World War II expansion of multinational business highlighted the need for consistent international rules. The League of Nations had already studied double taxation issues in the 1920s, but systematic transfer pricing guidance emerged only in the latter half of the 20th century. The Organization for Economic Co-operation and Development (OECD) became the central body in this effort. Its 1979 Transfer Pricing Guidelines formally endorsed the arm's length principle, providing methods such as comparable uncontrolled prices, resale price, and cost-plus to test related-party transactions. These guidelines set the global standard and were widely adopted by member and non-member countries alike.

Expansion and Refinement (1980s–2000s)

In the 1980s and 1990s, tax authorities observed increasing complexity in multinational operations, particularly with the rise of intangibles, intra-group services, and global financing structures. The United States responded with detailed regulations under Internal Revenue Code Section 482, finalized in 1994, which required extensive documentation and introduced advanced pricing methods, including the profit-split and comparable profits approaches. Other jurisdictions followed suit, enacting statutory documentation rules and penalties to deter profit shifting. The OECD revised its guidelines in 1995 to align with these developments, making the arm's length principle the globally accepted norm.

The Modern Era of Global Coordination

The 2000s and 2010s saw mounting concern over aggressive tax planning by multi-nationals, particularly in the digital economy. Public attention grew around cases where technology companies booked profits in low-tax jurisdictions. In response, the OECD launched the Base Erosion and Profit Shifting (BEPS) Project in 2013. BEPS Actions 8–10 refined the application of the arm's length principle to intangibles, risk allocation, and high-value services, while Action 13 introduced country-by-country reporting and standardized documentation requirements. These reforms significantly increased transparency and enabled tax authorities to better assess global profit allocations.

Current and Emerging Trends

Today, transfer pricing remains one of the most scrutinized areas of international taxation. The OECD's 2017 and 2022 updates have addressed profit splits, hard-to-value intangibles, and financial transactions. Simultaneously, the Two-Pillar Solution agreed to in 2021 marks a potential turning point: Pillar One reallocates taxing rights on the residual profits of large multinational enterprises, while Pillar Two introduces a global minimum tax. These initiatives suggest that transfer pricing may evolve beyond the arm's length principle, especially for digital and highly integrated business models.

Conclusion

From its beginnings as a domestic safeguard against income shifting in the 1920s, transfer pricing regulation has grown into a complex system of global rules. The arm's length principle remains the cornerstone, but increasing globalization and digitalization continue to challenge its adequacy. The future of transfer pricing is likely to be shaped by continued international cooperation, with reforms seeking both fairness in taxation and administrative feasibility.

The Objectives of Transfer Pricing Regulation

The primary objective of transfer pricing regulation is to ensure that transactions between related parties reflect prices consistent with those that would be agreed upon by independent entities operating under similar market conditions (the arm's length principle). This principle forms the foundation of most global frameworks and serves multiple regulatory, economic, and policy purposes. The following additional objectives are routinely mentioned by tax authorities in regard to transfer pricing:

- *Protection of tax revenue.* A central aim is to prevent profit shifting by multinational enterprises (referred to throughout the text as "multinationals"). Without regulation, multinationals could manipulate intercompany pricing to move profits into low-tax jurisdictions while allocating costs to high-tax countries, thereby eroding national tax bases. Transfer pricing rules safeguard government revenues by aligning taxable income with the real economic activities carried out within each jurisdiction.
- *Fairness and neutrality in taxation.* Regulation promotes fairness by ensuring that related-party transactions are taxed similarly to dealings between unrelated parties. This prevents multinationals from obtaining an unfair advantage over purely domestic firms that cannot shift profits across borders. By standardizing treatment, regulations uphold neutrality in competition and reinforce confidence in the tax system.
- *Alignment of profits with value creation.* Modern transfer pricing frameworks emphasize the principle that profits should be taxed where value is created. This is particularly important in industries involving intangibles, digital platforms, or integrated global supply chains. Regulation discourages artificial arrangements that misalign profits with real functions, assets, and risks.

- *Reduction of double taxation and disputes.* Clear transfer pricing rules and documentation requirements help minimize disputes between taxpayers and tax authorities. Moreover, consistent application across jurisdictions reduces the risk of *double taxation* (where two countries seek to tax the same income) by providing mechanisms such as advance pricing agreements and mutual agreement procedures (as discussed later in the text).
- *Promotion of transparency and compliance.* Documentation requirements, such as the OECD's country-by-country reporting under BEPS Action 13, improve transparency. They give tax authorities insight into global profit allocations and allow for more efficient risk assessment. This strengthens compliance and deters aggressive tax planning.
- *Facilitation of international cooperation.* Transfer pricing regulation encourages cooperation between tax authorities by providing standardized methods and principles. This harmonization promotes consistency in global tax enforcement and reduces uncertainty for businesses operating across borders.

In short, transfer pricing regulation aims to protect tax revenues, ensure fairness, align profits with economic substance, prevent double taxation, and foster transparency and cooperation. Together, these objectives support both the integrity of national tax systems and the stability of the international tax framework.

The Role of Transfer Pricing in International Taxation

Transfer pricing plays a pivotal role at the intersection of international taxation and the operations of multinationals. It governs the pricing of transactions between related entities across borders, including the transfer of goods, services, intellectual property, and financing. Because such intra-group dealings account for a significant share of global trade, transfer pricing directly influences how taxable profits are allocated among jurisdictions.

Transfer pricing regulation is one of the primary tools used by tax authorities to prevent base erosion and profit shifting. Without clear rules, multinationals could manipulate prices to allocate profits artificially to low-tax jurisdictions, undermining national tax bases. By applying the arm's length principle, international tax regimes seek to align reported profits with the economic substance of activities performed in each country. This ensures that taxation reflects genuine value creation and preserves fairness across jurisdictions.

Transfer pricing also interacts with broader international tax mechanisms. Disputes over profit allocation frequently lead to double taxation when two countries assert taxing rights over the same income. To address this, international frameworks promote consistent methodologies and offer dispute resolution mechanisms like mutual agreement procedures and advance pricing agreements. These tools help balance tax authority enforcement with the need for predictability in global commerce.

From the perspective of multinationals, transfer pricing is both a compliance requirement and a strategic tool. Companies must design intercompany pricing policies that meet regulatory standards while supporting internal goals such as cash flow management, performance measurement, and efficient global supply chain operation. Transfer pricing policies affect decisions on where to locate functions, how to structure intellectual property ownership, and how to finance cross-border operations. However, compliance costs and audit risks are significant. Multinationals must maintain detailed documentation and justify pricing decisions to tax authorities in multiple jurisdictions. Failure to comply can result in adjustments, penalties, and reputational damage.

In short, transfer pricing lies at the core of international taxation, determining how billions in corporate profits are allocated worldwide. For tax authorities, it safeguards revenue and fairness; for multinationals, it represents both a regulatory challenge and a central component of global business strategy.

Common Misconceptions and Challenges in Transfer Pricing

Transfer pricing is one of the most complex areas of international taxation, and both multinationals and tax authorities face persistent misconceptions and challenges in its application.

A widespread misconception is that transfer pricing is primarily a tax-avoidance scheme. While some multinationals have used aggressive pricing to shift profits, transfer pricing itself is a neutral concept that governs how related-party transactions should be priced. Its purpose is to ensure fairness, not necessarily to minimize taxes.

Another misconception is that applying the arm's length principle is straightforward. In reality, comparable uncontrolled transactions are often difficult to identify, especially in industries dominated by intangibles or unique business models. Some assume that financial ratios or profit splits can provide easy benchmarks, but these methods require extensive judgment and adjustments.

A further misunderstanding is that compliance only involves preparing documentation to satisfy regulators. In truth, transfer pricing is closely tied to strategic decisions, such as supply chain design, intellectual property ownership, and risk allocation, that affect both business performance and tax outcomes.

One major challenge is the valuation of intangibles. Intellectual property such as patents, trademarks, and algorithms often lacks reliable comparables, making it difficult to apply traditional pricing methods. This increases the risk of disputes and adjustments.

Another challenge is regulatory inconsistency. Although most countries follow OECD guidelines, interpretations vary, leading to conflicts between jurisdictions. This inconsistency exposes multinationals to the risk of double taxation and lengthy dispute resolution processes.

Administrative burden also poses difficulties. Companies must gather detailed data, conduct benchmarking studies, and maintain extensive documentation to justify transfer prices. These requirements are resource-intensive, particularly for smaller multinationals.

Finally, the rise of the digital economy has created new challenges. Digital platforms, data-driven value creation, and highly integrated global services often do not fit neatly into the arm's length framework, raising questions about whether traditional methods remain sufficient.

Misconceptions about transfer pricing, such as viewing it only as tax avoidance or assuming it is simple to apply, mask the real challenges of valuing intangibles, navigating inconsistent regulations, and handling heavy compliance demands. Addressing these issues requires both clearer international coordination and careful alignment of corporate strategy with regulatory expectations.

CASE STUDY

A well-known example of the challenges surrounding transfer pricing comes from disputes involving Apple Inc. and its Irish subsidiaries. Apple, like many multinational technology companies, centralized much of its intellectual property (IP) in low-tax jurisdictions. The company's European sales were often booked through Irish entities, which were subject to favorable tax treatment.

Tax authorities questioned whether Apple's transfer pricing practices appropriately reflected the value created in higher-tax jurisdictions where product development, marketing, and sales activities actually took place. Critics argued that profits allocated to Ireland were disproportionately high compared to the functions performed there. The European Commission eventually ruled that Ireland had granted Apple illegal state aid by allowing arrangements that artificially reduced its tax burden.

Challenges Highlighted

- *Valuing intangibles*. Apple's case underscored the difficulty of pricing IP such as brand reputation, patents, and proprietary technology. These assets were central to profit generation, but there were few reliable external comparables.
- *Jurisdictional inconsistencies*. While the European Commission focused on state aid rules, the U.S. tax authorities emphasized different aspects of transfer pricing under Section 482. This lack of alignment created uncertainty for Apple and risked double taxation.
- *Complex business models*. Apple's integrated global supply chain and centralized IP ownership highlighted how traditional arm's length methods struggle to capture the realities of modern multinational structures.
- *Public perception*. Beyond technical compliance, Apple faced reputational risks, as the public often equated transfer pricing strategies with tax avoidance, even though the arrangements were legal under certain interpretations of the rules.

This case illustrates how transfer pricing disputes are not only technical tax matters but also issues of public trust, corporate strategy, and international politics. It shows that relying heavily on low-tax jurisdictions for profit allocation can invite regulatory scrutiny and reputational damage.

Core Principles of Transfer Pricing

We have already noted that the primary source of transfer pricing guidelines has been produced by the OECD. While this is true, other entities have also produced transfer pricing guidelines, including the United Nations, the United States, India, China, and Australia. These guidelines may vary from each other, as discussed next.

OECD Transfer Pricing Guidelines

The OECD Transfer Pricing Guidelines are a cornerstone of international tax policy, designed to help multinational enterprises and tax authorities determine transfer prices for cross-border transactions. First issued in 1995 and updated multiple times (most significantly in 2017 as part of the Base Erosion and Profit Shifting project), the guidelines provide a framework for applying the arm's length principle.

What is the Base Erosion and Profit Shifting Project?

The Base Erosion and Profit Shifting (BEPS) Project is an initiative led by OECD and the G20 to address tax avoidance strategies used by multinational enterprises. These strategies exploit gaps and mismatches in international tax rules to shift profits to low- or no-tax jurisdictions, eroding the tax base of higher-tax countries. Launched in 2013, the BEPS Project produced a comprehensive 15-point action plan aimed at ensuring that profits are taxed where economic activities and value creation occur. Key measures include addressing harmful tax practices, preventing treaty abuse, aligning transfer pricing outcomes with value creation, and improving transparency through country-by-country reporting. The project has since evolved into the OECD/G20 Inclusive Framework, which brings together over 140 jurisdictions to implement and monitor BEPS measures. Its ultimate goal is to create a fairer, more transparent, and more consistent international tax system.

At their core, the guidelines emphasize the importance of comparability. They outline how to conduct a comparability analysis, considering factors such as contractual terms, functions performed, risks assumed, assets employed, and prevailing economic conditions. To implement this, the OECD identifies five traditional transfer pricing methods: Comparable Uncontrolled Price (CUP), Resale Price, Cost Plus, Transactional Net Margin Method (TNMM), and Profit Split (all discussed later in this course). These methods guide how profits and costs should be allocated across different jurisdictions to prevent the artificial shifting of taxable income.

The OECD also recognizes that modern business models, and especially those involving intangibles, services, and digital platforms, pose unique challenges. Consequently, the guidelines provide detailed instructions for valuing hard-to-price intangibles, allocating synergies from group arrangements, and addressing intra-group services. They stress that substance should prevail over form, meaning that the actual conduct of parties takes precedence over contractual labels when determining transfer prices.

From a compliance perspective, the guidelines recommend a three-tiered documentation structure: a master file providing an overview of global operations, a local file with country-specific details, and a country-by-country report disclosing financial and tax information across jurisdictions. This enhances transparency and enables tax administrations to better assess transfer pricing risks.

Ultimately, these guidelines seek to balance the interests of multinationals and tax authorities by promoting consistent, fair, and predictable outcomes. They reduce the likelihood of double taxation and disputes while curbing aggressive tax planning strategies. Although not legally binding, the guidelines have been widely adopted into domestic legislation and bilateral tax treaties, making them the de facto global standard for resolving transfer pricing issues in international taxation.

United Nations Practical Manual on Transfer Pricing

The United Nations Practical Manual on Transfer Pricing for Developing Countries is designed as a practical guide to help developing countries address the complexities of transfer pricing in a way that balances the needs of tax administrations and multinationals. While the OECD Transfer Pricing Guidelines serve as the global benchmark, the UN Manual provides an alternative perspective, incorporating the realities of countries with less administrative capacity and greater reliance on corporate tax revenues.

The Manual affirms the arm's length principle as the international standard, but it also discusses the challenges developing countries face in applying it, such as limited access to comparable data, weaker enforcement capacity, and asymmetries in negotiating with multinationals. It provides step-by-step guidance on performing a transfer pricing analysis, covering comparability, functional analysis, risk allocation, and the use of traditional methods. The Manual acknowledges that while the OECD approach is widely used, developing countries may require more flexible or simplified approaches in practice.

One of the distinctive features of the UN Manual is its practical orientation. It includes case studies, examples, and sector-specific discussions, such as on extractive industries and commodities (which are of high importance to many developing economies). It also addresses issues like management fees, intra-group services, and the use of safe harbors, which can ease compliance burdens. The Manual emphasizes dispute prevention and resolution, encouraging advance pricing agreements where feasible, and offering guidance on managing audits and minimizing double taxation.

Importantly, the UN Manual reflects a more balanced view of taxpayer and tax authority interests than the OECD guidelines, acknowledging the policy space of developing countries to adopt measures suited to their administrative realities. While it does not supplant the OECD Guidelines, it provides a complementary perspective that highlights fairness and simplicity.

Key U.S. Transfer Pricing Regulations

The United States has one of the most developed and influential transfer pricing regulatory frameworks, anchored in Internal Revenue Code Section 482 and the accompanying Treasury Regulations. Section 482 grants the Internal Revenue Service the authority to reallocate income, deductions, credits, or allowances among related parties to clearly reflect income and prevent tax evasion. The central standard applied is (as usual) the arm's length principle.

The Treasury Regulations under Section 482 provide detailed rules for determining appropriate transfer prices. They outline several approved methods, broadly aligned with OECD guidance: Comparable Uncontrolled Price (CUP), Resale Price, Cost Plus, Comparable Profits Method (CPM, the U.S. version of TNMM), and Profit Split. The "best method rule" requires taxpayers to use the method that provides the most reliable measure of an arm's length result, considering data quality and comparability.

The regulations also address intangibles, including intellectual property, which are critical to U.S. multinationals. Special rules govern cost-sharing arrangements, buy-in payments, and the valuation of hard-to-price intangibles. The IRS closely scrutinizes transfers of intangibles, given their potential for profit shifting. Similarly, services regulations provide simplified cost-based methods for routine services, while requiring arm's length pricing for higher-value services.

Compliance and documentation are central features of U.S. rules. Taxpayers must maintain contemporaneous documentation demonstrating that their transfer pricing policies are consistent with Section 482. Failure to provide adequate documentation can lead to significant penalties - up to 40% of the underpayment if the IRS deems the pricing to be substantially misaligned with arm's length standards.

To reduce disputes, the U.S. offers advance pricing agreements, allowing taxpayers and the IRS (and sometimes foreign authorities) to agree in advance on acceptable transfer pricing methods. Additionally, the U.S. participates in the mutual agreement procedure under tax treaties to resolve double taxation disputes arising from transfer pricing adjustments.

Overall, U.S. transfer pricing regulations are rigorous, emphasizing detailed economic analysis, robust documentation, and proactive compliance. They serve both as a revenue protection tool and as a global model, influencing the approaches of other countries while frequently being at the center of international tax controversies.

Other Regional Frameworks

Transfer pricing frameworks have evolved across regions to align with global standards while addressing local economic and administrative realities. For example, the European Union broadly adheres to the OECD Transfer Pricing Guidelines, but it also promotes regional consistency through initiatives like the EU Joint Transfer Pricing Forum (JTPF). The JTPF provides recommendations on documentation, dispute resolution, and advance pricing agreements, helping member states reduce double taxation and compliance burdens. The EU has also implemented country-by-country reporting as part of its anti-tax avoidance package, reinforcing transparency across member states.

Many Asia-Pacific countries have enacted detailed transfer pricing regulations inspired by the OECD framework, though with local adaptations. For instance, India emphasizes detailed documentation and places particular scrutiny on intangibles and service transactions, while China focuses on location-specific advantages and unique market conditions. Australia has been especially active in applying anti-avoidance rules alongside transfer pricing reviews. The region has also seen a rising use of APAs to provide certainty for taxpayers.

African countries increasingly recognize the revenue risks from transfer pricing, especially in resource-driven economies. The African Tax Administration Forum has developed transfer pricing guidelines tailored to local contexts, offering simplified approaches for commodity transactions and service arrangements. Countries such as South Africa, Nigeria, and Kenya have established robust rules, with a focus on documentation and related-party dealings in extractive industries.

Latin American countries often adopt OECD principles but also incorporate stricter, formula-based approaches. Brazil, for example, applies fixed margins rather than traditional OECD methods, providing simplicity but sometimes diverging from arm's length outcomes. Mexico, Chile, and Argentina follow OECD standards more closely, with strong documentation requirements. The region also emphasizes the exchange of information and aggressive enforcement to combat profit shifting.

Together, these regional frameworks illustrate a global convergence toward OECD standards, but with significant local variations reflecting policy priorities, administrative capacity, and economic structures.

Transfer Pricing Methods

There are five transfer pricing methods. In this section, we describe each one, along with any pertinent issues, and the circumstances under which they should be used.

Comparable Uncontrolled Price Method

The Comparable Uncontrolled Price (CUP) Method is one of the most direct and reliable transfer pricing methods endorsed by the OECD Transfer Pricing Guidelines and many national tax authorities. It determines the arm's length price of a controlled transaction by comparing it to the price charged in a comparable transaction between independent enterprises under similar circumstances. Because it relies on actual market prices, the CUP method is often considered the "gold standard" when truly comparable data are available. However, its applicability can be limited, as exact comparables are often difficult to find. Here are several areas of concern:

- *Product differentiation.* The most common problem is that the products being sold in the market are differentiated from each other by a variety of unique features, so there is no standard market price.
- *Quality differentiation.* Product features may be the same, but quality differences between products cause significant pricing differences.
- *Specialty products.* The components in question may be of such a highly specialized nature that there is no market for them at all.
- *Internal costs.* The cost of selling internally to another subsidiary is somewhat lower than the cost of selling to an external customer, since there are fewer selling costs and bad debts associated with an internal sale; this means that comparing potential sales based just on the market price is not correct.

- *Corporate planning.* If there is a centralized planning staff, they may not want the subsidiaries to make decisions based on the market price, because they want all components routed to internal subsidiaries to relieve supply shortages. This is not necessarily a problem, as long as the internal sales are conducted at the market price.

The CUP method evaluates whether the amount charged in a controlled transaction (between related parties, such as parent and subsidiary) aligns with the price charged in a comparable uncontrolled transaction (between independent parties). The comparability assessment considers factors such as:

- Product or service characteristics – including quality, specifications, and functions.
- Contractual terms – such as delivery conditions, payment terms, and volume.
- Economic circumstances – including market conditions, geographic location, and timing.
- Business functions and risks – whether parties bear similar levels of risk and contribute equivalent assets or intangibles.

If material differences exist, adjustments are required to improve comparability. For example, price adjustments might reflect differences in credit terms, volumes purchased, or delivery conditions.

EXAMPLE

Assume ParentCo, based in the United States, sells a patented pharmaceutical ingredient to its subsidiary SubCo in Brazil. ParentCo charges SubCo $500 per kilogram. To evaluate whether this price meets the arm's length standard, the tax authority looks for comparable uncontrolled transactions.

Through market research, they identify that ParentCo also sells the same pharmaceutical ingredient to an unrelated distributor in Canada at $520 per kilogram, under nearly identical conditions (same product, similar volume, and similar contractual terms). The only notable difference is that sales to Canada include a 60-day credit period, while sales to Brazil require payment within 30 days. After adjusting for the time value of money (say, a 2% adjustment), the Canadian price is effectively $510 per kilogram on a comparable basis.

Comparing the adjusted CUP price ($510) with the controlled transaction price ($500), the transfer price to SubCo is slightly lower. However, the difference falls within an acceptable arm's length range, so the transaction is considered compliant.

The CUP method provides a clear and defensible approach to transfer pricing when identical or highly similar transactions exist in the open market. Its strength lies in its reliance on observable market prices. The main challenge is the scarcity of reliable comparables, particularly for unique products, intangibles, or intra-group services.

Where available, however, CUP offers the most precise benchmark for ensuring compliance with the arm's length principle.

Resale Price Method

The Resale Price Method (RPM) is one of the traditional transaction methods used in transfer pricing to determine whether the price charged between related parties is consistent with the arm's length principle. It is particularly suitable for distributors or resellers who purchase goods from a related party and then resell them to an independent third party without significant value-adding activities.

Under RPM, the starting point is the resale price charged by the reseller to an unrelated customer. From this resale price, an appropriate gross margin (comparable to that earned by independent distributors performing similar functions under similar conditions) is deducted. The resulting figure represents the arm's length purchase price that the distributor should have paid to its related supplier.

The method focuses on gross margins rather than net margins because distribution functions (such as warehousing, marketing, or sales support) can be benchmarked against independent distributors. It is most reliable when the reseller does not significantly alter the goods, such as in consumer goods distribution or wholesale trading.

EXAMPLE

Grouch Electronics, a U.S. parent company, manufactures smartphones and sells them to its wholly owned subsidiary, Grumpy Distributors, located in Germany. Grumpy resells the smartphones in the German market to unrelated retailers. It follows these steps to determine the appropriate transfer price under the resale price method:

- *Step 1*. Resale price to third parties. Grumpy sells the smartphones to retailers for €500 each.
- *Step 2*. Determine appropriate gross margin. Comparable independent distributors in Germany earn a gross margin of 25% on similar products. This margin compensates the distributor for its functions (sales, marketing, logistics) and risks (inventory risk, credit risk).
- *Step 3*. Compute arm's length purchase price. The resale price is €500, less the arm's length gross margin of 25% (calculated as €500 × 25%). The arm's length transfer price = €375.

Thus, the transfer price that Grouch should charge Grumpy for each smartphone is €375. This ensures that Grumpy earns an arm's length gross margin of €125 per unit.

If Grouch had instead charged Grumpy only €300 per unit, Grumpy's gross margin would be €200 (40%), which is above the industry benchmark and would suggest profit shifting into Germany. Conversely, if Grouch charged €450, Grumpy's margin would shrink to €50 (10%), below the arm's length range, raising concerns that profits are being shifted back to the U.S.

The resale price method is a practical approach for evaluating transfer pricing in distribution scenarios. By anchoring the analysis on the resale price to independent customers and benchmarking gross margins, RPM ensures that the reseller's profitability aligns with what independent entities would achieve in comparable market conditions.

Cost-Plus Method

The cost-plus method of transfer pricing is one of the traditional transaction-based approaches recognized under the OECD Transfer Pricing Guidelines. It establishes the transfer price by starting with the costs incurred by the supplier of goods or services in a controlled transaction, and then adding an appropriate mark-up to account for profit. This method is particularly useful when semi-finished goods are sold between related parties, or when group members provide services or contract manufacturing. Its main goal is to ensure that the transfer price reflects an arm's length return for the supplying entity, consistent with what independent firms would negotiate under comparable circumstances.

The process begins with identifying the supplier's direct and indirect costs associated with producing the good or service. These costs typically include raw materials, labor, and overhead. A mark-up is then applied, derived from comparable transactions between unrelated parties. This margin is critical, because it ensures that the supplier earns a fair return without shifting excessive profits within the multinational group. The reliability of the method depends heavily on the availability of appropriate comparables, especially regarding mark-ups in similar industries and functions.

EXAMPLE

Assume Company A, a subsidiary in Mexico, manufactures electronic components exclusively for its parent company, Company B, located in the United States. Company A's total production cost for one unit is $100, including materials, labor, and overhead. To determine the transfer price using the cost-plus method, a mark-up must be applied. An analysis of comparable independent manufacturers shows that third-party suppliers in the electronics industry typically apply a 20% gross profit mark-up on costs. In this case, the transfer price per unit is calculated as:

- Cost of production: $100
- Mark-up (20% × $100): $20
- Transfer price: $120

Thus, Company A would charge Company B $120 per unit. This ensures that Company A earns an arm's length profit, while Company B receives the components at a price comparable to what it would have paid in an open market.

The strength of the cost-plus method lies in its simplicity and direct connection to actual costs. However, it may be less reliable in highly specialized industries where cost structures vary significantly or when appropriate comparables for mark-up percentages are scarce. Despite these challenges, it remains an important method for ensuring compliance with transfer pricing regulations and avoiding profit shifting disputes.

Transactional Net Margin Method

The Transactional Net Margin Method (TNMM) is a widely used transfer pricing method under the OECD Transfer Pricing Guidelines. It evaluates whether the pricing of transactions between related parties is arm's length by comparing the net profit margin earned in controlled transactions to that earned by independent enterprises engaged in similar activities under comparable circumstances. Unlike the Comparable Uncontrolled Price method, which looks at prices directly, or the Resale Price/Cost Plus methods, which focus on gross margins, TNMM examines the net operating margin relative to an appropriate base such as sales, costs, or assets.

The method relies on identifying a tested party, usually the entity with the least complex functions and risks, and calculating its net margin indicator. This margin is then compared with those of comparable independent companies (derived from commercial databases or market analysis). Adjustments may be required to improve comparability, particularly for differences in accounting classifications, functions, or market conditions.

TNMM is advantageous when no reliable internal or external comparable prices exist, as it tolerates broader comparability differences. However, its reliance on net margins makes it less precise than transaction-based methods, since operating margins can be influenced by many non-transfer pricing factors such as management efficiency, cost structures, and local market conditions.

EXAMPLE

A multinational has a subsidiary in Country A that distributes consumer electronics imported from its parent company in Country B. The subsidiary performs routine distribution functions, including warehousing, marketing, and after-sales support, while the parent retains responsibility for product design, branding, and strategic marketing.

The tax authority in Country A examines whether the distributor's profitability reflects an arm's length result. The distributor's operating margin (operating profit divided by sales) is calculated at 2%. To benchmark this, the multinational's advisors search for independent distributors of similar electronics in Country A. After screening, they identify a set of five comparable companies, which show net margins ranging from 3% to 6%, with an interquartile range of 3.5% to 5.5%.

Since the subsidiary's 2% margin falls below the arm's length range, an adjustment is required. To align with the lower end of the interquartile range (3.5%), the transfer price of the goods purchased from the parent must be reduced. This adjustment increases the distributor's operating profit, ensuring compliance with the arm's length principle.

TNMM is a practical and widely accepted transfer pricing method, particularly when detailed comparable transaction data is unavailable. Its focus on net margins makes it flexible but also less precise than transaction-based methods. In practice, it is often applied to routine functions such as distribution and contract manufacturing, ensuring that these entities earn an arm's length return consistent with comparable independent firms.

Profit Split Method

The profit split method is a transfer pricing approach used to allocate profits (or losses) among related entities engaged in cross-border transactions. It is particularly appropriate when the activities of the parties are so integrated that they cannot be evaluated on a standalone basis, or when each party contributes unique and valuable intangibles. Rather than comparing transactions to external benchmarks, the method seeks to divide the combined profit of the transaction in a way that reflects each party's relative contributions.

Under this method, the first step is to identify the total combined profit from the intercompany transaction. This profit is then split between the associated enterprises using either a contribution analysis or a residual analysis. In a *contribution analysis*, profits are divided based on the relative value of functions performed, assets used, and risks assumed by each party. In a *residual analysis*, routine returns are first allocated to each party based on standard industry benchmarks, and the remaining residual profit (typically linked to unique intangibles) is then shared according to their relative contributions.

The profit split method is especially relevant in industries such as technology, pharmaceuticals, and financial services, where interdependencies and unique intangible assets make it difficult to apply traditional comparable-based methods. It reduces the risk of one entity capturing disproportionate profits from integrated global activities.

EXAMPLE

There is a multinational pharmaceutical company where the U.S. parent develops new drug compounds, while its Swiss subsidiary handles large-scale manufacturing and distribution in Europe. Both entities contribute significantly; the parent through R&D and intellectual property, and the subsidiary through specialized production facilities and market access.

The combined profit from the sale of a new drug in Europe is $200 million. Using a residual profit split approach, routine functions such as manufacturing and distribution are allocated standard returns of $40 million to the Swiss subsidiary, while routine R&D support is allocated $20 million to the U.S. parent. This leaves a residual profit of $140 million, attributable to the unique intangible contributions of both parties.

An analysis shows that the U.S. parent's patents and ongoing R&D efforts contribute 70% of the residual value, while the Swiss subsidiary's specialized facilities and regulatory expertise contribute 30%. Therefore, the split allocates $98 million to the U.S. parent and $42 million to the Swiss subsidiary. Thus, the final allocation is as follows:

U.S. parent = $118 million ($20m + $98m), Swiss subsidiary = $82 million ($40m + $42m).

In this way, the profit split method ensures that both entities are rewarded in proportion to their real economic contributions, reflecting the arm's length principle when comparable transactions are unavailable.

Selecting the Most Appropriate Method

Selecting the most appropriate transfer pricing method is a critical decision for multinational enterprises because it determines how income and expenses are allocated among related entities in different tax jurisdictions.

The selection process begins with a functional analysis, which examines the functions performed, assets employed, and risks assumed by each entity involved in the transaction. This analysis helps determine the relative contributions of the parties and whether comparables exist in the marketplace. For example, a routine distribution subsidiary taking limited risks may be best analyzed under the resale price or cost-plus methods, while two parties both contributing unique intangibles may require the profit split method.

Next, companies must consider the availability and reliability of comparable data. The comparable uncontrolled price (CUP) method is generally preferred if high-quality comparable transactions between independent parties can be identified. However, in industries with unique products or proprietary intangibles, reliable comparables are often scarce, pushing taxpayers toward transactional profit methods such as the transactional net margin method (TNMM) or profit split. Regulators typically favor methods that use the most reliable data and minimize assumptions.

Taxpayers also need to evaluate the nature of the transaction. For tangible goods, CUP, resale price, or cost-plus methods may be most suitable. For services, the cost-plus or TNMM approaches are commonly applied, while transactions involving intangibles often require profit split or residual approaches. The complexity of integration between related parties further influences the choice: highly integrated operations make it difficult to isolate each party's contribution, making the profit split approach more appropriate.

Another factor is consistency with industry practice. Certain industries, such as financial services or commodities trading, may have well-established norms for pricing transactions, which authorities expect companies to follow. At the same time, taxpayers must account for regulatory preferences in each jurisdiction, since some countries give priority to particular methods.

Ultimately, the most appropriate method is the one that, given the facts and circumstances, provides the most reliable measure of an arm's length result. Taxpayers are expected to document the rationale behind their selection, demonstrating why alternatives were rejected. A well-supported choice not only ensures compliance but also reduces the risk of disputes with tax authorities.

FRAMEWORK FOR SELECTING A TRANSFER PRICING METHOD

Step 1: Define the Transaction Clearly
- Identify the nature of the controlled transaction (tangible goods, services, intangibles, financing).
- Map the parties involved and the flow of goods, services, or funds.

Step 2: Conduct a Functional Analysis
- Document functions performed, assets used, and risks assumed by each entity.
- Determine whether one party is a routine service provider/distributor or if both contribute unique intangibles.

Step 3: Assess Availability of Comparables
- Search for internal comparables (transactions with unrelated parties under similar conditions).
- If not available, search for external comparables in databases, industry reports, or public filings.
- Evaluate quality: Are the comparables sufficiently similar to support CUP, resale price, or cost-plus?

Step 4: Match Method to Transaction Type
- Tangible goods: Start with CUP (if good comparables exist), otherwise consider resale price or cost-plus.
- Services: Often suited for cost-plus or TNMM.
- Intangibles: If unique and valuable, consider profit split; otherwise use CUP.
- Highly integrated operations: Profit split may be most reliable.

Step 5: Evaluate Reliability of Data
- Ask: Which method uses the most reliable data available?
- Prioritize methods that minimize assumptions and adjustments.
- Exclude methods where data gaps would lead to weak results.

Step 6: Consider Industry and Regulatory Expectations
- Align with common industry practice (e.g., CUP for commodities, TNMM for low-risk distributors).
- Factor in local tax authority preferences (many regulators view CUP as first priority).

Step 7: Apply the "Most Appropriate Method" Principle
- Select the method that best reflects arm's length pricing under the facts and data available.
- Justify why other methods are less reliable for the specific transaction.

Step 8: Document the Rationale
- Provide a clear explanation of why the method was chosen.
- Include details of the functional analysis, comparables search, and rejected alternatives.
- This documentation is critical for defending the method in audits.

Comparability Analysis

One of the primary analysis tasks in transfer pricing is comparability. In this section, we cover the factors impacting comparability, the concepts of internal and external comparables, the data sources for comparables, and several related issues.

Factors Affecting Comparability

In transfer pricing analysis, *comparability* refers to the degree to which transactions between related parties can be reliably compared to those between independent parties. The accuracy of an arm's length determination largely depends on how well the chosen comparables reflect the conditions of the controlled transaction. Several factors influence comparability, including the following items:

- *Characteristics of the goods or services.* The physical features, quality, and volume of goods, or the nature of services provided, directly affect pricing. For instance, commodity transactions may lend themselves to direct comparisons under the CUP method, while highly customized products with unique features make comparability more difficult.
- *Functional analysis.* The functions performed, assets employed, and risks assumed by each party are central to comparability. Two entities may sell the same product, but if one bears greater market risk or invests heavily in marketing intangibles, their pricing structures will differ. Accurately aligning functional profiles ensures more reliable comparisons.
- *Contractual terms.* Written agreements regarding payment terms, credit periods, warranties, exclusivity, and rights to intangibles can materially impact prices. Even if the goods or services are similar, differences in contractual obligations may undermine comparability.
- *Economic circumstances.* Market conditions, geographic location, competitive environment, and business cycles all affect comparability. For example, the same product may command different prices in emerging markets compared to mature economies due to purchasing power, demand, or local regulations.
- *Business strategies.* Corporate strategies, such as market penetration pricing, product differentiation, or long-term growth plans, can justify deviations in pricing from what would otherwise appear comparable. For instance, a subsidiary may temporarily accept lower margins to establish market share.
- *Data availability and reliability.* The quality of available information on independent transactions determines the reliability of comparables. In some industries, public data is scarce, forcing reliance on broader ranges of comparables or less direct methods like TNMM.

These factors are described in the following exhibit.

In practice, perfect comparability is rare. Adjustments are often made to account for differences in functions, risks, or economic conditions, but excessive adjustments reduce reliability. Ultimately, comparability depends on identifying transactions where differences do not materially affect the outcome, ensuring that the arm's length principle is applied fairly and consistently.

Comparability Factors in Transfer Pricing

Factor	Description	Example
Characteristics of goods or services	Physical features, quality, and type of goods/services affect comparability.	A generic drug vs. a patented drug cannot be directly compared under CUP.
Functional analysis	Functions performed, assets used, and risks assumed by each party must align.	A full-risk distributor vs. a limited-risk distributor will show different margins.
Contractual terms	Legal agreements on credit, exclusivity, warranties, or rights impact pricing.	A distributor with exclusive regional rights may accept lower margins.
Economic circumstances	Market conditions, geography, and business cycles influence outcomes.	The same machinery sold in the U.S. vs. an emerging market may differ in price.
Business strategies	Long-term goals like penetration pricing or differentiation affect comparability.	A company may sell at a loss initially to capture market share.
Data availability	Reliable, high-quality data on independent transactions improves comparability.	Publicly traded companies provide better comparables than private firms.

Internal vs. External Comparables

In transfer pricing, comparables are independent transactions used to test whether related-party dealings are consistent with the arm's length principle. These comparables fall into two categories: internal comparables and external comparables, each with distinct advantages and limitations.

Internal comparables arise when a multinational engages in the same or similar transactions with both related and unrelated parties. For example, if a company sells identical products to independent distributors and also to its subsidiary, the prices charged to the independent distributors provide an internal comparable. Internal comparables are generally considered more reliable because the data is directly available to the taxpayer, involves the same products, and reflects similar business practices. They also reduce the need for broad assumptions or adjustments, since differences in functions, risks, and markets can be evaluated with firsthand knowledge. However, internal comparables are not always available, especially in cases involving unique intangibles or specialized services offered only within the group.

External comparables involve transactions between two independent enterprises, neither of which is part of the multinational group. These are often identified through commercial databases, industry reports, or publicly available financial statements. External comparables are crucial when no internal comparables exist, such as in industries where all sales are conducted within the group. While external comparables provide a broader benchmark, their reliability is often limited by data constraints. Publicly available information may not reveal detailed functional profiles, contractual terms, or risk allocations, necessitating adjustments that reduce accuracy.

The choice between internal and external comparables depends on availability and reliability. Tax authorities and the OECD Guidelines generally prefer internal comparables, since they are closer to the controlled transaction. When only external comparables exist, taxpayers must carefully demonstrate how they are sufficiently similar, or make justified adjustments for differences.

In practice, both types of comparables play essential roles. Internal comparables, when available, often provide the strongest evidence for arm's length pricing. External comparables broaden the scope of analysis and are particularly useful for industries with standardized products or services, such as commodities, financial instruments, or distribution margins. A well-supported transfer pricing analysis typically starts with internal comparables and only relies on external ones when no suitable internal benchmarks exist.

Data Sources for Comparables

In transfer pricing analysis, the reliability of the arm's length outcome depends heavily on the quality of data sources used to identify comparables. Since comparability requires transactions between independent parties under similar conditions, companies and tax authorities rely on a mix of internal and external data sources to benchmark controlled transactions. The main sources are as follows:

- *Internal company data.* The first source of comparables is often within the multinational itself. If the company engages in the same type of transaction with independent third parties, such as selling the same product to both related and unrelated distributors, those transactions provide strong internal comparables. Internal data is highly reliable, because it reflects the company's actual pricing policies, product specifications, and risk structures.

- *Commercial databases.* When internal comparables are unavailable, external databases are the most common source of information. These include global financial and transactional databases such as Orbis, Amadeus, Compustat, Capital IQ, RoyaltyStat, ktMINE, and Bloomberg, which provide access to financial statements, royalty agreements, loan terms, and distributor margins. These databases allow practitioners to build sets of comparable companies or transactions, particularly for TNMM, CUP, or profit split analyses. However, reliability depends on data quality and the adjustments needed for differences in functions, geography, or timing.

- *Publicly available information.* Annual reports, stock exchange filings, industry publications, and government filings often disclose information on pricing, margins, and licensing arrangements. For example, SEC filings may reveal related-party royalty rates or intercompany loan terms. Industry benchmarks, market surveys, and trade publications can also provide valuable insights.

- *Government and regulatory sources.* Some governments maintain databases of independent royalty rates, customs valuations, or industry pricing reports.

For instance, the U.S. Securities and Exchange Commission or the European Patent Office can provide licensing information, while customs data may serve as a benchmark for goods pricing.

- *Industry-specific data.* Specialized industries often have proprietary sources of comparables. For commodities, market price indexes (e.g., Platts, Metal Bulletin) serve as CUP comparables. In financial services, central bank publications or loan market data may establish independent benchmarks. For intellectual property, databases of licensing agreements (e.g., RoyaltySource, ktMINE) provide comparables for royalty rates.

The characteristics and applicability of these data sources are noted in the following exhibit.

In practice, analysts prioritize internal data where available, and use external sources to supplement or validate results. Each source requires careful screening and adjustments to ensure the comparables reflect the arm's length principle, balancing availability with reliability.

Data Sources for Comparables in Transfer Pricing

Data Source	Description	Typical Use Cases
Internal company data	Transactions between the multinational and independent third parties.	Sales of the same goods/services to unrelated customers; distributor margins.
Commercial databases	Subscription-based global databases.	TNMM benchmarking (profit margins), CUP for loans/royalties, distributor studies.
Public filings and reports	Annual reports, SEC filings, stock exchange disclosures, industry surveys.	Royalty rates, intercompany loan terms, industry margin benchmarks.
Government sources	Customs data, tax authority publications, patent office databases.	Customs values for goods, licensing arrangements, statutory pricing data.
Industry-specific sources	Specialized market indexes and trade publications.	CUP for commodities, market pricing of raw materials, industry-standard service fees.
Royalty/license databases	Databases of IP licensing agreements.	CUP for intangibles, benchmarking royalty rates for trademarks, patents, software.
Financial market data	Loan and bond market data, central bank reports, yield curves.	CUP for intercompany financing, interest rate benchmarking.

Adjustments for Differences

In transfer pricing analysis, even the best comparables rarely match controlled transactions perfectly. Differences in functions, risks, markets, or contract terms can materially affect prices and margins. To achieve a reliable arm's length result, adjustments are often required so that the comparables more closely resemble the tested transaction. These adjustments, however, must be reasonable, well-documented, and not so extensive that they undermine the reliability of the comparison. The most common adjustments are as follows:

- *Accounting adjustments.* Financial data may differ due to varying accounting standards (e.g., IFRS vs. U.S. GAAP) or policies on depreciation, inventory valuation, or revenue recognition. Adjustments normalize these differences so that margins and ratios are comparable across entities.
- *Working capital adjustments.* Companies with different levels of receivables, payables, or inventories incur different financing costs. A distributor with longer credit terms to customers will show lower margins compared to one with faster collections. Adjusting for differences in working capital aligns profitability measures, especially under the TNMM.
- *Capacity utilization adjustments.* Entities operating at different capacity levels may report distorted cost structures. For instance, underutilized plants allocate higher fixed costs per unit, lowering profitability. Adjusting for normal or expected utilization improves comparability in manufacturing sectors.
- *Risk adjustments.* Independent entities may assume different levels of market, credit, or product liability risk than related parties. If the tested party is a limited-risk distributor, adjustments may be required when comparing it to full-risk distributors. These adjustments ensure that profits reflect only the risks borne.
- *Geographic adjustments.* Prices and margins vary significantly across regions due to differences in purchasing power, competition, or regulation. Adjustments for geographic markets are common, especially when using external comparables from countries with different economic conditions.
- *Functional adjustments.* When comparables perform additional functions, such as marketing, R&D, or after-sales service, adjustments are made to strip out the returns related to those activities. This isolates the margin attributable to the tested party's actual functions.
- *Extraordinary items.* Events such as litigation expenses, restructuring charges, or one-time windfalls can distort profitability. Excluding extraordinary items ensures that only recurring business results are compared.

Ultimately, adjustments must improve comparability without introducing excessive subjectivity. If too many or too significant adjustments are needed, the comparables may not be reliable, and another method or dataset should be considered. Proper adjustments, when carefully applied, increase the defensibility of a transfer pricing analysis and strengthen compliance with the arm's length principle.

EXAMPLE

A U.S. subsidiary of a multinational acts as a limited-risk distributor of consumer electronics. To test whether its operating margin is consistent with the arm's length principle under the Transactional Net Margin Method (TNMM), the company identifies a set of independent distributors as comparables.

The tested subsidiary reports an operating margin of 3.5%. The comparables show an average margin of 5%, suggesting that the subsidiary may be underpriced. However, further analysis reveals a significant difference in working capital levels.

The tested subsidiary extends 90-day credit terms to its customers to promote sales, leading to an average accounts receivable balance equal to 25% of sales. By contrast, the independent comparables extend only 30-day credit terms, with receivables averaging 10% of sales. This means the tested party bears higher financing costs and liquidity risks than the comparables, depressing its margin.

A working capital adjustment is made to neutralize this difference. Analysts calculate the excess receivables (15% of sales) and apply a 6% interest rate to determine the financing cost burden. On sales of $100 million, this adjustment amounts to $0.9 million, which is added back to the subsidiary's operating profit.

After adjustment, the subsidiary's margin rises from 3.5% to 4.4%, narrowing the gap with the comparables' 5% margin. This demonstrates that, once differences in working capital are accounted for, the controlled transaction aligns more closely with the arm's length range.

Benchmarking Studies and Statistical Tools

In transfer pricing, benchmarking studies and statistical tools are essential for supporting the arm's length nature of related-party transactions. They provide objective evidence by comparing controlled results with those of independent enterprises engaged in similar activities.

A *benchmarking study* is a systematic process of identifying and analyzing comparable companies or transactions to establish an arm's length range of results. Practitioners typically use commercial databases to select independent companies or licensing arrangements similar to the tested party. Screening criteria are applied to filter potential comparables, such as industry classification, geographic region, size, and functional profile.

The outcome is a set of comparable companies or transactions whose financial ratios (such as operating margin, return on total costs, or royalty rates) form the benchmark range. The tested party's results are then compared against this range. If the tested result falls within the arm's length range, the transfer price is considered compliant. If it falls outside, adjustments may be required. Benchmarking studies are particularly common when applying methods like the transactional net margin method or the comparable uncontrolled price for royalties and loans.

Because comparable data often varies significantly, statistical tools help refine the analysis. The most common approach is using the interquartile range (25th to 75th percentile) rather than the full range, which reduces the influence of outliers. Measures such as the median or weighted average are also used to represent the arm's length point within the range.

In some cases, regression analysis or correlation studies may be employed to test relationships between profitability and variables like working capital or sales volume, improving the robustness of the comparability analysis. Sensitivity analysis is also applied to assess how changes in assumptions affect results.

Together, benchmarking studies and statistical tools enhance the credibility, objectivity, and defensibility of transfer pricing analyses, ensuring that results are consistent with the arm's length principle and acceptable to tax authorities.

EXAMPLE

A French subsidiary of a multinational operates as a limited-risk distributor of household appliances. The parent company in Germany supplies products, while the French entity handles only local sales and distribution. The goal is to determine whether the French subsidiary's operating margin aligns with the arm's length principle.

Step 1: Define the tested party and method. The French distributor is chosen as the tested party because its functions are less complex than the German parent. The transactional net margin method is applied, using the operating margin (Operating Profit/Sales) as the profit level indicator.

Step 2: Identify comparables. A benchmarking study is conducted using the Orbis database. Screening criteria are applied, as follows:

- Industry codes (distributors of durable goods)
- European region
- Similar turnover size
- Exclusion of companies with persistent losses or unrelated activities

This yields 12 independent distributors as comparables.

Step 3: Conduct a statistical analysis. The operating margins of the 12 comparables range from 1% to 9%. To avoid distortion by extreme values, the interquartile range is calculated, as follows:

- 25th percentile: 3%
- Median: 5%
- 75th percentile: 7%

Step 4: Compare results. The French subsidiary reports an operating margin of 4.8%. This lies comfortably within the interquartile range of 3%–7%, demonstrating compliance with the arm's length principle.

By combining a structured benchmarking study with a statistical tool, the company shows that its transfer pricing arrangement is consistent with independent market results. This evidence can be documented and presented to tax authorities, thereby strengthening the defensibility of its pricing policy.

Intra-Group Transactions

Certain types of transfer pricing arrangements can be especially troublesome for the accountant. In the following pages, we address the issues associated with the transfer of tangible goods, services, and intangible assets, and also delve into the issues arising from cost sharing arrangements.

Tangible Goods Transactions

Tangible goods transactions are the most common type of intra-group dealings subject to transfer pricing rules. They involve the sale or transfer of physical products between the entities of the same multinational that are located in different tax jurisdictions. Because tangible goods are traded extensively across borders, these transactions form the backbone of many transfer pricing analyses.

Key comparability factors for tangible goods include product characteristics (quality, specifications, and brand), contractual terms (volume discounts, credit periods, and warranties), and economic conditions (geography, market demand, and competition). Adjustments are often required to account for differences, such as freight costs or customs duties, when comparing intra-group and third-party prices.

Ultimately, analyzing tangible goods transactions in transfer pricing is about balancing precision with practicality: using the best available comparables and methods to ensure that profits are allocated fairly among jurisdictions while reflecting the commercial reality of the group's operations.

EXAMPLE

A German parent company manufactures specialized electronic components. It sells these components both to independent European customers and to its wholly owned subsidiary in Poland, which assembles them into finished products for resale in Eastern Europe. The key pricing information is as follows:

- Independent sales price (to third parties): €100 per unit (FOB Germany)
- Intra-group sales price (to subsidiary): €92 per unit

At first glance, the intra-group price seems lower, raising concerns about whether it complies with the arm's length principle. However, closer analysis reveals that the terms of sale differ, as noted below:

- Independent customers purchase in small batches of around 500 units per order.
- The subsidiary purchases in bulk; typically 5,000 units per shipment.
- Bulk purchasers usually receive discounts in this industry. Market research shows that discounts of 7–10% are common for orders of this size.

Applying an adjustment for volume differences, the comparable uncontrolled price can be re-stated as follows:

- Independent price (€100) minus average 8% volume discount = €92 per unit.

This adjusted CUP shows that the intra-group transfer price of €92 per unit is fully consistent with what an independent customer would have paid under similar circumstances.

Services Transactions

In transfer pricing, intra-group service transactions arise when one entity within a multinational provides services to another related entity. Because services often lack tangible outputs or direct market comparables, determining an arm's length charge can be complex. To address this, the OECD Guidelines and many tax authorities distinguish between low value-adding services and high value-adding services, each subject to different transfer pricing considerations. They are as follows:

- *Low value-adding services.* These are routine support functions that are ancillary to the main business activities and do not materially contribute to the group's core value creation. Examples include accounting, payroll, human resources, IT support, and general administrative assistance. Since these services typically do not involve unique intangibles or significant risk, they are charged using a simplified cost-based method. The OECD allows the application of a cost-plus markup (often around 5%) to recover costs and provide a modest profit, reducing compliance burdens and disputes. Tax authorities generally view these as eligible for simplified documentation, provided companies can demonstrate that the services were actually rendered and benefited the recipient.
- *High value-adding services.* In contrast, high value-adding services directly contribute to the multinational's core profit-generating activities. These include research and development, strategic management, product design, marketing intangibles, and financial advisory services. Because such services often involve unique know-how, intellectual property, or significant risks, they cannot be priced using simple markups. Instead, methods such as the comparable uncontrolled price or profit split are more appropriate. These services require robust benchmarking studies, as their value can vary widely across industries and circumstances.

The distinction is crucial: low value-adding services benefit from administrative simplification, while high value-adding services demand detailed analysis and stronger documentation. Proper classification helps multinationals allocate costs fairly, comply with transfer pricing rules, and reduce the risk of challenges by tax authorities.

Intangible Assets

When intangible assets are transferred within a multinational group, they present some of the most complex challenges in transfer pricing. Intangibles (such as patents, trademarks, copyrights, software, customer lists, or proprietary know-how) are often unique and not easily comparable to third-party transactions. Because of this, the valuation and pricing of intra-group transfers of intangibles must comply with the arm's length principle while reflecting the particular economic contributions of each party involved.

The OECD Transfer Pricing Guidelines emphasize that the first step is to identify the intangible itself and determine which entity within the group is the legal owner and which entities perform functions that enhance, maintain, or protect the intangible. For example, a parent company may hold the legal title to a patent, but a subsidiary may conduct significant R&D activities that create or enhance its value. In such cases, both legal ownership and functional contributions must be taken into account to ensure that the entity performing the development functions is adequately compensated.

Pricing intangibles in intra-group transactions typically requires more than standard methods such as the comparable uncontrolled price, since external benchmarks are often unavailable. Instead, approaches such as profit split methods or valuation techniques like discounted cash flow are applied, taking into consideration the expected future economic benefits of the intangible. For instance, if a subsidiary is granted rights to use a trademark in a particular jurisdiction, the transfer price should reflect the projected revenues attributable to that brand in that market.

Another critical aspect is the distinction between "hard-to-value" intangibles and those with established market comparables. Tax authorities are especially cautious of situations where intangibles are transferred at an early development stage at low valuations, only for the asset to generate substantial profits later. In these cases, adjustments may be made retrospectively to ensure that the pricing reflects the actual economic outcome rather than an undervalued forecast.

Overall, the treatment of intangible assets in intra-group transactions involves balancing legal ownership with the economic reality of value creation, applying transfer pricing methods that capture future profit potential, and aligning outcomes with the arm's length principle. This makes intangible asset transfers among the most scrutinized and contentious areas in transfer pricing.

EXAMPLE

The parent company of a multinational develops a proprietary software platform in the United States. The parent legally owns the intellectual property (the software code and related patents). However, much of the enhancement and localization of the software for international markets is carried out by a subsidiary in Germany, which employs skilled developers and contributes significantly to the platform's commercial success in Europe.

The U.S. parent licenses the software to the German subsidiary for distribution in the European market. If the transaction were treated as a simple license, the parent might charge a royalty rate based only on comparable license agreements it finds in the market. However, such comparables are rare because the software is unique, and the German subsidiary is adding significant value through its own development work. Applying only a market-based royalty might undervalue the German subsidiary's contribution and shift too much profit to the parent.

To resolve this, the multinational's accountants instead apply a profit split method. The combined European revenues from the software are first identified, and then the profits are allocated between the U.S. parent and the German subsidiary based on each party's functions, assets, and risks. The parent, as the legal owner and originator of the software, receives a larger share for its initial R&D and continuing ownership of the IP, while the German subsidiary is allocated a meaningful share for its ongoing development and market-specific adaptations.

In practice, this allocation could be supported with a discounted cash flow valuation of the intangible, estimating how much of the future profits are attributable to the parent's initial innovation versus the subsidiary's ongoing enhancements. This way, the intra-group transaction reflects both the legal and the economic reality, ensuring that each entity is compensated at arm's length for its contributions to the intangible's value.

Cost Sharing Arrangements

Cost sharing arrangements are treated as intra-group transactions in transfer pricing because they involve the allocation of costs and risks among related parties within a multinational. Under these arrangements, group members agree to share the costs of developing, producing, or acquiring assets, services, or rights, with the expectation that each participant will benefit from the resulting intangibles or services in proportion to its contributions. This makes them distinct from ordinary service transactions, as the arrangement is forward-looking and tied to anticipated benefits rather than immediate services rendered.

From a transfer pricing perspective, tax authorities require that these arrangements meet the arm's length standard. Each participant's share of costs must be consistent with the share of expected benefits it will receive, and contributions can be made in cash or in kind, such as through existing technology, know-how, or services. If a participant does not contribute in proportion to its expected benefits, the shortfall is treated as a deemed transfer from another participant, and must be compensated with an arm's length payment. This ensures that one entity is not effectively subsidizing another without proper recognition of value, which would otherwise distort the taxable income allocation within the group.

Documentation and compliance are critical in these intra-group cost sharing arrangements. The OECD Transfer Pricing Guidelines and U.S. regulations set detailed requirements for defining participants, determining costs to be shared, valuing intangible contributions, and periodically adjusting allocations to reflect changes in anticipated or actual benefits. The treatment aligns the arrangement with broader transfer pricing principles, emphasizing that intra-group transactions must mirror what independent enterprises would have agreed upon in comparable circumstances.

In essence, cost sharing arrangements are viewed as a structured form of intra-group transfer pricing, designed to allocate the burden of developing valuable intangibles or services fairly across the entities that benefit.

EXAMPLE

A multinational group has two subsidiaries, which are USCo (located in the United States) and EUCo (located in Germany). They decide to enter into a cost sharing arrangement to jointly develop new enterprise software. Both companies will use the software in their respective markets. The related transfer pricing activities are as follows:

Step 1: Estimate expected benefit shares. The group projects that USCo will generate 60% of the global revenues from the software, while EUCo will generate 40% of the revenues. Thus, the expected benefit shares are 60% for USCo and 40% for EUCo.

Step 2: Identify total costs to be shared. The annual R&D budget for developing the software is $10 million.

Step 3: Allocate costs in proportion to expected benefits:

- USCo's share = 60% × $10 million = $6 million
- EUCo's share = 40% × $10 million = $4 million

Step 4: Contributions:

- USCo actually incurs $7 million in direct R&D expenses.
- EUCo actually incurs $3 million in direct R&D expenses.

Step 5: Adjustments for imbalance. USCo contributed $7 million but its required share is only $6 million, so it over-contributed by $1 million. EUCo contributed $3 million but its required share is $4 million, so it under-contributed by $1 million. To restore balance, EUCo must make a balancing payment of $1 million to USCo.

This $1 million payment is treated as an intra-group transaction and must comply with the arm's length principle. The adjustment ensures that each subsidiary bears costs in proportion to its expected benefits, as unrelated parties would do in a joint development agreement.

Common Errors in Transfer Pricing Analysis

Errors in transfer pricing analysis often arise because of the complexity of intercompany transactions, the subjectivity involved in valuing intangibles, and the challenges of applying the arm's-length principle consistently across multiple jurisdictions. These errors can undermine both compliance and defensibility during audits.

One of the most frequent mistakes is the selection of inappropriate comparables. Analysts may use companies that are not truly similar in functions, assets, and risks, leading to distorted benchmarking results. For example, including firms that operate in different geographic markets, with different risk profiles, or in unrelated product segments can skew arm's-length ranges. Closely related to this error is the failure to adjust comparables properly. Differences in working capital, accounting policies, or market conditions often require adjustments, but companies sometimes omit these refinements, producing misleading conclusions.

Another common problem lies in the misapplication of transfer pricing methods. Firms may default to a method that favors their tax position rather than one that best reflects the transaction's economic reality. For example, using a transactional net margin method where reliable comparable uncontrolled prices are available can appear manipulative. Regulators increasingly expect companies to justify not only why a method was chosen but also why other methods were rejected.

A further error is the reliance on outdated or incomplete data. Many analyses use historical financials or static comparables that no longer reflect current market conditions. Because transfer pricing disputes often focus on specific years, a failure to use contemporaneous data weakens a taxpayer's defense. Similarly, omitting key intercompany transactions (such as service fees, royalties, or cost allocations) from the analysis creates an incomplete picture that tax authorities can easily challenge.

Documentation lapses represent another major source of error. Companies sometimes prepare transfer pricing studies as a compliance formality, without ensuring that the underlying data reconcile with financial statements or that the narrative accurately describes functional responsibilities. Discrepancies between reported policies and actual practices can be exploited by tax auditors. This disconnect can also appear in multinational groups that apply different methodologies in different jurisdictions, leading to inconsistent narratives.

Finally, many errors stem from undervaluing or mischaracterizing intangibles. Assigning little or no profit to entities that develop or maintain intellectual property, or attributing excessive returns to holding companies with minimal substance, has been a recurring source of controversy. The OECD's BEPS reforms specifically target these practices, and failing to adapt analyses accordingly exposes companies to significant adjustment risks.

In short, common errors in transfer pricing analysis include the use of inappropriate comparables, inadequate adjustments, misapplication of methods, reliance on outdated data, incomplete transaction coverage, weak documentation, and the mischaracterization of intangibles. Each of these weaknesses not only jeopardizes compliance but also undermines the company's ability to defend its pricing policies under increasing global scrutiny.

A practical checklist of red flags that tax authorities often look for when reviewing transfer pricing analyses includes the following items:

- *Inconsistent profit levels.* Subsidiaries operating in high-tax jurisdictions consistently report very low or negative profits while affiliates in low-tax countries show disproportionately high margins. This pattern suggests profit shifting and is an immediate red flag.
- *Inappropriate comparables.* Benchmarking studies include companies that differ significantly in size, geography, industry, or risk profile from the tested party. Tax authorities are quick to challenge analyses where comparables are not economically similar.
- *Lack of adjustments.* Analyses present raw financial ratios without making adjustments for working capital, capacity utilization, or accounting policy

differences. The absence of reasonable adjustments raises doubts about whether the arm's-length standard has truly been applied.

- *Selective method application.* The company relies on one method, such as TNMM, despite the availability of a more reliable method like CUP or resale price. Authorities treat selective method choice as a sign of results-driven analysis rather than objective compliance.

- *Outdated or non-contemporaneous data.* Benchmark studies use financials that are several years old or do not align with the audited period under review. Regulators generally expect contemporaneous data that reflect the exact fiscal year.

- *Weak or generic documentation.* The transfer pricing file lacks detailed functional analysis, risk allocation, or explanations of why certain methods were chosen. Vague or boilerplate documentation is a red flag that policies are not grounded in the company's actual business model.

- *Mischaracterization of intangibles.* Entities in low-tax jurisdictions are assigned ownership of valuable intangibles but perform little or none of the development, enhancement, maintenance, protection, or exploitation (DEMPE) functions. This disconnect is heavily scrutinized.

- *Discrepancies with financial statements.* Figures used in the transfer pricing analysis do not reconcile with statutory accounts or consolidated financial statements. Inconsistencies in reported numbers will erode a firm's credibility.

- *Unexplained year-to-year variability.* Profit margins, transfer pricing methods, or comparables change significantly from one year to the next without clear business reasons. Authorities view sudden changes as opportunistic tax planning.

- *Absence of local file or master file alignment.* Local files submitted in one jurisdiction are inconsistent with the master file (as discussed in the next section) or with files submitted elsewhere. Differences across countries invite tax authority cooperation under OECD BEPS exchange-of-information frameworks.

This checklist represents the typical red flags that auditors and regulators look for when deciding whether to challenge a transfer pricing study. Addressing these proactively strengthens both compliance and defensibility in audits.

Documentation and Compliance

The OECD's transfer pricing rules have led to the adoption of a common set of documentation standards that multinationals are expected to comply with. In the following pages, we discuss the standard documentation package, as well as local variations from this standard, and best practices for preparing the documents.

OECD Three-Tiered Documentation Standard

The OECD's Three-Tiered Documentation Standard was introduced as part of the Base Erosion and Profit Shifting Project, to provide tax administrations with greater transparency regarding multinationals' global operations and transfer pricing practices. The objective is to ensure that tax authorities can better assess whether intercompany transactions comply with the arm's length principle, while also balancing the compliance burden for taxpayers. The framework consists of three distinct components, which are as follows:

- The *Master File* provides a high-level overview of a multinational's global business operations, transfer pricing policies, and allocation of income and economic activity. It is designed to give tax administrations a clear understanding of how the group as a whole operates, where its key profit drivers are located, and how intangible assets, financing, and supply chains are structured. Typical contents include descriptions of the organizational structure, business activities, intangibles, intercompany financial arrangements, and consolidated financial results. This broad perspective helps authorities place local transactions in the proper global context.
- The *Local File* is far more detailed and specific to each individual jurisdiction. It focuses on the material intercompany transactions of the local entity and provides supporting evidence that those transactions are consistent with the arm's length principle. Contents generally include descriptions of the local entity's management structure, detailed analyses of intercompany transactions, functional and risk assessments, transfer pricing methods used, and financial information relevant to the local taxpayer. This enables tax authorities to directly evaluate whether the transfer prices applied in their jurisdiction are appropriate.
- The *Country-by-Country Report* adds a quantitative layer by requiring large multinationals to provide annual aggregate data on income, taxes paid, and economic indicators such as employees and tangible assets for each jurisdiction in which they operate. This report is not intended to serve as a direct basis for transfer pricing adjustments but as a risk assessment tool for tax authorities, allowing them to identify mismatches between reported profits and the economic activities conducted in various countries.

Together, the three tiers provide a balanced system: the Master File sets the global scene, the Local File substantiates arm's length compliance at the local level, and the Country-by-Country Report provides transparency for risk assessment. This layered approach ensures that tax administrations have sufficient information to challenge inappropriate transfer pricing outcomes, while still maintaining proportional compliance requirements for taxpayers. Highly summarized sample reports appear in the following exhibits.

SAMPLE MASTER FILE

Organizational Structure

Anterior Group is a multinational enterprise headquartered in the Netherlands. The group operates through subsidiaries in 25 countries, with key operations in North America, Europe, and the Asia-Pacific region. The parent company, Anterior Holding B.V., owns all operating subsidiaries. An organizational chart outlining legal ownership and principal entities is provided in Appendix A.

Description of the Business

Anterior Group develops, manufactures, and sells consumer electronics and software solutions. The group's primary business lines include (1) smartphones, (2) home automation devices, and (3) enterprise cloud software. Anterior pursues an integrated business model where research and development (R&D) is centralized in Germany and the United States, while manufacturing is located in China and Vietnam. Distribution and marketing functions are handled by regional subsidiaries.

Global demand for consumer electronics is highly competitive, with innovation and brand recognition being critical profit drivers. The group invests heavily in R&D to maintain its technological leadership.

Intangibles

The group's key intangible assets include patents on smartphone technology, proprietary software code, and valuable trademarks (e.g., the "Anterior" brand). Legal ownership of patents and trademarks is held by Anterior IP B.V. in the Netherlands, which licenses these rights to operating subsidiaries. Development, enhancement, maintenance, protection, and exploitation (DEMPE) functions are performed mainly in Germany (software development) and the United States (hardware R&D).

Intercompany Financial Arrangements

Anterior Group uses a centralized treasury entity, Anterior Finance Ltd. in Ireland, which provides funding to subsidiaries through intercompany loans. The treasury entity also manages cash pooling and hedging activities for foreign exchange risks. Intercompany financing is priced at arm's length using comparable uncontrolled loan data.

Financial and Tax Position

Anterior Group's consolidated revenue for its most recent fiscal year was €20 billion, with operating profits of €3.2 billion. The largest markets were the United States (35% of revenues), Germany (20%), and China (15%). A summary of consolidated financial statements is attached in Appendix B.

SAMPLE LOCAL FILE

1. Introduction and Company Overview
Entity Name: Posterior, Inc.
Jurisdiction: United States
Ownership: 100% owned by Anterior Holdings Ltd. (headquartered in the Netherlands)
Business Description: Posterior develops, manufactures, and distributes network hardware for enterprise clients in North America. It also provides limited R&D support services for the group.

2. Management and Organizational Structure
Board of Directors: Local representation with oversight from Global HQ.
Management: Day-to-day operations are led by US-based executives in sales, marketing, and operations.
Reporting: Posterior reports financial and operational results directly to Global HQ.

3. Description of Controlled Transactions
3.1 Purchase of Components from Related Party
Counterparty: Sunset Corporation (manufacturing affiliate in Malaysia)
Transaction Value: $75 million
Nature of Transaction: Purchase of networking components for final assembly and resale.
Transfer Pricing Method Applied: Comparable Uncontrolled Price, benchmarked against third-party purchase agreements.

3.2 Provision of R&D Services
Counterparty: Anterior Holdings Ltd.
Transaction Value: $12 million
Nature of Transaction: Contract R&D services performed by US engineers.
Transfer Pricing Method Applied: Cost Plus Method, applying a 7% markup on costs, consistent with comparables.

3.3 Payment of Royalties for Technology License
Counterparty: Anterior IP Ltd. (Ireland)
Transaction Value: $18 million
Nature of Transaction: Licensing of proprietary technology used in hardware products sold in North America.
Transfer Pricing Method Applied: Transactional Net Margin Method, with a target royalty rate based on industry benchmarks (5% of net sales).

4. Functional Analysis
Functions Performed: Sales, marketing, limited R&D, final assembly.
Assets Used: Tangible assets (assembly facilities, warehouses), licensed intangibles (patents, trademarks).
Risks Assumed: Market risk, inventory risk, limited product liability risk.

5. Benchmarking Analysis
R&D Services: Benchmark study identified comparable U.S. engineering firms providing contract R&D, with an interquartile markup range of 5%–9%. Posterior's 7% markup falls within this range.

Royalty Payments: Benchmarking study of third-party licensing agreements in the tech sector showed royalty rates between 4%–6% of net sales. Posterior's 5% rate is consistent with these arm's length transactions.

6. Financial Information
Posterior Revenues: $300 million
Operating Profit: $32 million (10.7% margin)
Transfer Pricing Adjustments: None required, as results were within the arm's length range.

SAMPLE COUNTRY-BY-COUNTRY REPORT

Table 1 – Overview of Allocation of Income, Taxes, and Business Activities by Tax Jurisdiction

Tax Jurisdiction	Revenues Unrelated Party ($M)	Revenues Related Party ($M)	Total Revenues ($M)	Profit Before Tax ($M)	Income Tax Paid ($M)	Income Tax Accrued	Stated Capital ($M)	Accum. Earnings ($M)	Number of Employees	Tangible Noncash Assets
United States	300	25	325	32	8.0	9.0	150	220	550	90
Malaysia	20	75	95	12	2.0	2.5	50	40	800	110
Ireland	10	18	28	20	2.2	2.5	10	45	75	15
Netherlands	5	0	5	3	0.5	0.5	100	150	60	20
Total	335	118	453	67	12.7	14.5	310	455	1,485	235

Table 2 – List of Constituent Entities Included in Each Tax Jurisdiction

Tax Jurisdiction	Constituent Entities	Main Business Activities
United States	Posterior, Inc.	Sales, distribution, limited R&D, final assembly
Malaysia	Sideways Inc.	Manufacturing of networking components
Ireland	Anterior IP Ltd.	Ownership and licensing of intellectual property
Netherlands	Anterior Holdings Ltd.	Group headquarters, strategic management, financing

Table 3 – Additional Information

- **Intercompany Transactions:**
  - Posterior purchased components worth $75m from Sideways Inc.
  - Posterior paid $18m in royalties to Anterior IP Ltd.
  - Posterior received a $12m payment for R&D services provided to Anterior Holdings.

- **Transfer Pricing Policies:**
  - Component purchases benchmarked under CUP method.
  - R&D services priced on a Cost Plus basis with a 7% markup.
  - Royalty payments based on TNMM benchmarking at 5% of net sales.

- **Tax Risk Considerations:**
  - The group ensures that cost sharing and royalty payments align with arm's length principles.
  - No material transfer pricing adjustments were made in the most recent fiscal year.

Essentials of Transfer Pricing

35

Local Variations in Documentation Standards

Local variations in transfer pricing documentation rules arise because, although the OECD has established a standardized three-tiered framework, individual jurisdictions implement these requirements differently depending on their legal systems, administrative capacities, and policy priorities. While the OECD framework provides the foundation, national rules often diverge in terms of scope, format, thresholds, and filing procedures, creating significant compliance complexity for multinationals.

One key variation is in thresholds for documentation. The OECD recommends that Country-by-Country Reports apply to multinationals with consolidated revenues of at least €750 million. While many countries have adopted this threshold, others have set lower ones to capture more groups, while some impose additional conditions such as local filing if the parent jurisdiction does not exchange reports. Similarly, materiality thresholds for Local File documentation differ widely, with some countries requiring reports for all intercompany transactions and others only for transactions exceeding a certain monetary value.

Another difference lies in the format and content requirements. While the OECD prescribes general categories of information, local authorities often impose more detailed specifications. For example, some countries demand disclosure of detailed financial data on the comparables used in benchmarking, while others require industry-specific information such as descriptions of supply chains, location savings, or the detailed analysis of intangibles. China, for instance, emphasizes location-specific advantages and "value creation" in its documentation rules, while India requires the detailed disclosure of "specified domestic transactions." In contrast, some smaller jurisdictions adopt lighter rules, focusing only on basic transfer pricing policies.

Filing and language requirements also vary considerably. Some jurisdictions mandate contemporaneous documentation that must be available at the time of filing the corporate tax return, while others only require it upon request during an audit. In the European Union, many countries require filings in the local language rather than in English, adding a translation burden. Moreover, deadlines differ: in some countries documentation must be filed with the tax return, while in others it must simply be kept on hand.

Finally, penalties for non-compliance vary significantly. Certain countries impose severe monetary penalties, or even deny tax deductions for undocumented related-party payments. Others adopt more flexible approaches, imposing penalties only if transfer pricing adjustments are ultimately made.

Overall, while the OECD framework has created a measure of global consistency, multinationals must still navigate a patchwork of national rules. This reality means that transfer pricing compliance is not just about aligning with the arm's length principle, but also about tailoring documentation to the unique requirements of each jurisdiction in which the group operates.

Best Practices in Transfer Pricing Documentation

Best practices in transfer pricing documentation revolve around producing information that is not only compliant with regulatory requirements but also defensible in the event of a tax audit. Because transfer pricing remains one of the most frequently challenged areas of multinational taxation, documentation must strike a balance between technical rigor, transparency, and practicality.

One best practice is to anchor documentation in the arm's length principle with clear evidence. This means conducting robust functional and risk analyses that show which entities perform core functions, bear risks, and use key assets. The narrative should not be generic, but tailored to the realities of the business, ensuring that the transfer pricing methods selected are credibly linked to the company's commercial behavior. Authorities often scrutinize inconsistencies, so aligning the description of value creation with financial results is critical.

Another important practice is to ensure consistency across the three OECD tiers of documentation, which are the Master File, Local File, and Country-by-Country Report. Discrepancies between global narratives, local transaction-level detail, and aggregated jurisdictional data are a common source of challenges. Best practice dictates a coordinated documentation process in which global and local teams collaborate to reconcile differences before filing.

The use of reliable benchmarking studies is also central. Comparables must be selected using a transparent and defensible process, with clear criteria for inclusion and exclusion. Documenting adjustments for differences in comparables (such as working capital or geographic factors) helps strengthen credibility. Companies should refresh their benchmarking analyses periodically to reflect market changes and maintain relevance.

Contemporaneous preparation is another best practice. Authorities in many jurisdictions require that documentation be prepared by the time the tax return is filed. Even where not mandated, having documentation ready and up to date before an audit begins reduces risks and demonstrates good faith. A reactive approach, by contrast, often leaves gaps and inconsistencies that auditors exploit.

It is also advisable to maintain a forward-looking perspective. Documentation should not only describe past results but also anticipate how pricing policies will apply under changing business conditions, such as restructurings, supply chain adjustments, or evolving regulatory environments. The proactive inclusion of explanations for volatility or one-off results helps avoid later disputes.

Finally, centralized oversight with local adaptation is crucial. A global transfer pricing policy provides coherence, but documentation must be adapted to meet local variations in rules, thresholds, and language requirements. Central oversight ensures consistency, while local tailoring addresses jurisdiction-specific demands.

In sum, the best practices in transfer pricing documentation combine technical precision, internal coordination, and proactive compliance. When executed properly, documentation not only mitigates tax risk but also strengthens the alignment of tax and business strategy.

Dispute Resolution and Risk Management

Multinationals are routinely embroiled in transfer pricing controversies. In the following pages, we discuss the most common causes of these controversies, as well as transfer pricing audits, risk mitigation practices, and the use of advance pricing agreements and mutual agreement procedures to minimize conflicts with tax authorities.

Common Transfer Pricing Controversies

Transfer pricing controversies are among the most common sources of disputes between multinationals and tax authorities. They arise because transfer pricing sits at the intersection of taxation, economics, and corporate strategy, and involves significant judgment in applying the arm's length principle. Several recurring themes have made transfer pricing a perennial source of controversy worldwide.

One of the most frequent controversies involves the valuation of intangibles. Intellectual property such as patents, trademarks, and proprietary technology is often developed in one jurisdiction but exploited in many others. Determining where the value is created, and how much compensation is owed across entities, is highly subjective. Disputes often focus on whether royalties are set at arm's length, whether "buy-in" payments for cost-sharing arrangements are adequate, or whether location-specific advantages have been properly recognized. Countries like the U.S., India, and China frequently audit intangible-related transactions because of their large impact on taxable income.

Another source of conflict is the allocation of risk among group entities. Multinationals often characterize certain subsidiaries as "limited-risk distributors" or "contract manufacturers," justifying lower profit margins in those jurisdictions. Tax authorities sometimes challenge this classification, arguing that the local entity actually assumes greater risks, such as inventory or market risk, and therefore should earn a higher return. This can lead to disputes over whether the functional analysis matches the economic reality.

The choice of transfer pricing method is another common flashpoint. Taxpayers may favor methods that yield lower taxable income in high-tax jurisdictions, while tax authorities may argue that alternative methods are more appropriate. For example, disagreements often occur between using the Comparable Uncontrolled Price method versus a profit-based method like the Transactional Net Margin Method. The lack of perfect comparables exacerbates these conflicts.

Controversies also frequently arise in relation to intra-group financing. Intercompany loans, guarantees, and cash pooling arrangements are scrutinized to determine whether interest rates or guarantee fees are at arm's length. Thin capitalization rules and OECD guidance on financial transactions have made this an increasingly contentious area, especially where low-tax jurisdictions host finance companies.

Finally, Country-by-Country Reporting mismatches have become a new source of disputes. Tax authorities now have unprecedented visibility into where profits and taxes are reported relative to employees and tangible assets. Where profits appear misaligned with economic activity, authorities often initiate audits, even if the taxpayer has robust transfer pricing documentation.

In essence, transfer pricing controversies stem from the tension between taxpayer discretion in setting prices and tax authorities' mandate to protect their revenue base. These disputes are costly, protracted, and sometimes involve double taxation if multiple jurisdictions assert conflicting claims. For this reason, multinationals increasingly rely on advance pricing agreements and mutual agreement procedures (as discussed later) to mitigate controversy risk.

CASE STUDY

GlaxoSmithKline, the UK-based pharmaceutical giant, faced one of the largest transfer pricing cases in U.S. history. The controversy centered on how much profit from U.S. sales of block-buster drugs should be attributed to the U.S. distributor (GlaxoSmithKline U.S.) versus the UK parent company. The U.S. argued that the U.S. subsidiary performed significant marketing functions and bore market risks, entitling it to a larger share of profits. GSK countered that the high profitability was due to valuable patents and R&D developed in the UK.

The case was settled in 2006, with GSK agreeing to pay $3.4 billion to the IRS, one of the largest transfer pricing settlements ever. This case highlights disputes over the relative importance of marketing intangibles versus technological intangibles in profit allocation.

Audits and Adjustments by Tax Authorities

Audits and adjustments by tax authorities are central to the enforcement of transfer pricing rules. Because transfer pricing directly affects how much profit is taxed in each jurisdiction, authorities devote considerable resources to scrutinizing intercompany transactions. For multinationals, transfer pricing audits can be time-consuming, costly, and disruptive, often resulting in significant adjustments and the risk of double taxation.

The audit process usually begins with a risk assessment, often triggered by Country-by-Country Reports, local filings, or unusual patterns in tax returns. Authorities look for mismatches between the profits reported in a jurisdiction and the economic activity occurring there, such as sales, employees, or tangible assets. Industries with high levels of intangibles, complex supply chains, or frequent intercompany services are especially prone to scrutiny.

Once selected for audit, tax authorities typically demand extensive documentation to support the taxpayer's transfer pricing arrangements. This includes the Master File, Local File, benchmarking studies, intercompany agreements, and financial statements. A common point of contention is whether the chosen transfer pricing method is appropriate, or whether another method would yield a more reliable result. Authorities also challenge assumptions in benchmarking studies, such as the selection of comparables or the adjustments applied.

If authorities conclude that transfer prices are not consistent with the arm's length principle, they will issue an adjustment, reallocating profits within the group. For example, a tax authority may increase the taxable income of a local subsidiary by raising the deemed arm's length price of goods purchased from an affiliate. Adjustments often carry not only additional tax liabilities but also penalties and interest charges, with the severity varying by jurisdiction.

A major risk is double taxation, since the counterparty jurisdiction may not accept the corresponding downward adjustment. This can create prolonged disputes where the same income is taxed twice. Mechanisms such as the Mutual Agreement

Procedure under tax treaties, or bilateral and multilateral Advance Pricing Agreements provide ways to resolve or prevent these conflicts, but they are resource-intensive and may take years to conclude.

Ultimately, transfer pricing audits and adjustments highlight the tension between taxpayer discretion and government revenue protection. For multinationals, the best defense lies in thorough contemporaneous documentation, well-reasoned economic analyses, and proactive risk management strategies, including the use of advance pricing agreements where appropriate.

CASE STUDY

Anterior Holdings Ltd. operates through several subsidiaries, which are Posterior, Inc. in the United States (sales, distribution, limited R&D, and final assembly), as well as Sideways Inc. in Malaysia (manufactures networking components) and Anterior IP Ltd. in Ireland (holds patent and license intangibles).

The following transactions occurred during the company's most recent fiscal year:

- Posterior purchased $75m of components from Sideways Inc.
- Posterior paid $18m in royalties to Anterior IP for technology use.
- Posterior performed R&D services worth $12m for headquarters on a cost-plus 7% basis.
- Posterior reported revenues of $300m and operating profit of $32m (10.7% margin).

The parent entity's Country-by-Country Report shows the following:

- Posterior employs 550 staff but reports only 10.7% margins.
- Anterior IP in Ireland, with 75 staff, reports profit of $20m on only $28m revenues.
- Sideways Inc. in Malaysia employs 800 staff but shows relatively modest profits.

Given this information, United States auditors would reasonably question whether profits are realistically aligned with functions and risks. The company's tax manager would likely have to defend why the CUP method was chosen to develop transfer prices for components, whether the 5% royalty on net sales is realistically at arm's length, and whether the 7% markup on R&D comparable is reasonable. Depending on how the tax manager responds, the auditors might reasonably expect to reduce the amount of deductible royalties being recognized by Posterior, which would increase the subsidiary's taxable income.

Advance Pricing Agreements

Advance pricing agreements (APAs) are formal arrangements between a multinational and one or more tax authorities that establish, in advance of actual transactions, an agreed-upon method for determining transfer prices. The primary objective of an APA is to provide certainty and predictability regarding transfer pricing treatment, thereby reducing the risk of disputes, double taxation, and costly litigation. APAs are particularly important in transfer pricing because the valuation of cross-border intra-group transactions is highly subjective, and different tax authorities may adopt conflicting positions. By obtaining an APA, taxpayers and governments align on how transfer pricing rules will apply to specific transactions for a set period of time.

There are three main types of APAs: unilateral, bilateral, and multilateral. A unilateral APA involves only the taxpayer and the tax authority of its home jurisdiction, but it may leave the taxpayer exposed to adjustments by foreign tax authorities. Bilateral and multilateral APAs, by contrast, involve the tax authorities of two or more countries and are generally preferred because they reduce the risk of double taxation. In practice, bilateral APAs are negotiated under the mutual agreement procedures (as discussed in the next section) provided by tax treaties, ensuring that both sides accept the agreed pricing method.

The APA process typically involves a thorough examination of the taxpayer's business operations, the functions performed, risks assumed, and assets employed by different group entities. The taxpayer submits a detailed proposal to the tax authority, including functional and economic analyses, comparability studies, and justification for the proposed pricing method. Negotiations follow, often requiring extensive back-and-forth discussions and additional data requests. Once finalized, the APA sets forth the agreed methodology for calculating transfer prices over a specified period, usually ranging from three to five years, though extensions are possible.

From the perspective of multinational enterprises, APAs provide substantial benefits. They eliminate uncertainty, reduce exposure to transfer pricing adjustments, and lower the risk of penalties or double taxation. APAs also improve relations with tax authorities by demonstrating good faith and transparency. For tax authorities, APAs reduce the administrative burden of audits and disputes, while promoting compliance and encouraging cooperation with taxpayers. However, the APA process can be costly and time-consuming, requiring significant resources for documentation, negotiation, and monitoring compliance with the terms of the agreement.

Despite these challenges, APAs are widely regarded as one of the most effective tools for managing transfer pricing risk. Their role has expanded with the increasing focus on international tax compliance, particularly under the OECD's BEPS framework, which emphasizes transparency and consistency in global tax practices. As cross-border business transactions become more complex, APAs are likely to remain a central mechanism for reconciling the interests of taxpayers and tax authorities in the realm of transfer pricing.

Mutual Agreement Procedures

Mutual agreement procedures, often referred to as MAPs, are dispute resolution mechanisms provided under bilateral tax treaties to address issues of double taxation and inconsistent tax treatment, particularly in the context of transfer pricing. Because transfer pricing relies heavily on subjective judgments regarding the allocation of income and expenses among related entities, it is one of the most common sources of disputes between tax authorities in different jurisdictions. When two countries apply their transfer pricing rules to the same transaction in conflicting ways, the result can be double taxation of the same income. The MAP process provides a structured framework for resolving such disputes by allowing the tax authorities of the countries involved to negotiate an agreement.

The MAP process is typically initiated by a taxpayer who believes that taxation imposed by one or both countries is not in accordance with the provisions of the applicable tax treaty. The taxpayer must submit a request to the tax authority in its country of residence, usually within a time frame specified by the treaty, which is often three years from the first notification of the taxation in question. Once accepted, the tax authority reviews the case, consults with the taxpayer, and communicates with its counterpart in the other country to determine whether the double taxation can be eliminated or alleviated.

Transfer pricing cases under MAP often involve complex economic analyses and a deep understanding of the business operations of the multinational requesting the review. Each authority must assess the functions, risks, and assets of the group entities involved, review comparables, and consider whether the pricing method applied is consistent with the arm's length principle. The discussions can take considerable time, frequently extending over several years, due to the technical complexity of the issues and the need for both countries to protect their respective tax bases.

The outcome of a MAP is an agreement between the tax authorities rather than a unilateral decision, which means that both sides must compromise to achieve a resolution. Once an agreement is reached, the tax authorities will adjust the tax assessments accordingly, ensuring that the income is only taxed once. For taxpayers, this provides relief from double taxation and brings a level of certainty that might not be possible through domestic legal remedies alone. Importantly, the taxpayer is usually required to accept the MAP outcome in full, and in many cases must agree to forgo domestic appeals if the MAP process is pursued to completion.

Mutual agreement procedures are closely connected to advance pricing agreements, since bilateral APAs are negotiated through the same treaty-based framework as MAPs. While APAs are prospective, setting transfer pricing rules in advance, MAPs are retrospective, resolving disputes after they have arisen. Both mechanisms, however, reflect the increasing need for cooperation and coordination among tax authorities in a world where multinationals operate across multiple jurisdictions. The MAP process remains a vital tool for maintaining fairness and consistency in the international tax system, despite challenges such as lengthy timelines, resource demands, and varying levels of commitment among countries to fully implement the agreements reached.

Litigation vs. Settlement Strategies

Litigation and settlement represent two contrasting strategies available to multinationals and tax authorities when disputes arise over transfer pricing. Both approaches are shaped by the inherent complexity and subjectivity of transfer pricing, where differences in the interpretation of the arm's length principle can lead to significant adjustments and potential double taxation. The choice between pursuing litigation or seeking settlement depends on considerations of risk, cost, timing, and the broader relationship between the taxpayer and the tax authority.

Litigation is typically the last resort in transfer pricing disputes. When a taxpayer and a tax authority cannot reach agreement through audits, negotiations, or mutual agreement procedures, the dispute may proceed to court or an administrative tribunal.

Litigation offers the advantage of providing a definitive, legally binding decision that clarifies how the law should be applied in a given situation. For taxpayers, this may create precedent and protect them from recurring challenges in the future. However, litigation is often costly, protracted, and uncertain. Courts may lack the technical expertise to evaluate complex transfer pricing analyses, relying instead on competing expert testimony, which can lead to unpredictable outcomes. Additionally, litigation may strain relationships with tax authorities, potentially inviting greater scrutiny of future transactions.

Settlement, by contrast, involves negotiation and compromise between the taxpayer and the tax authority outside of court. This approach emphasizes pragmatism, seeking a resolution that avoids the expense and uncertainty of litigation. Settlement discussions may take place during or after the audit stage, and can result in reduced adjustments, phased compliance obligations, or other concessions that mitigate the impact of the original tax authority position. Taxpayers often favor settlement because it provides faster resolution, reduced risk, and the ability to preserve working relationships with tax officials. Tax authorities may also prefer settlement because it conserves administrative resources and avoids the possibility of an unfavorable outcome.

The choice between litigation and settlement is rarely clear-cut. A taxpayer facing an unreasonable or aggressive adjustment that could influence future assessments may decide that litigation, despite its risks, is preferable to compromise. Conversely, when financial exposure is manageable and the taxpayer values certainty and speed, settlement becomes the more rational option. Increasingly, companies adopt a blended strategy (resolving disputes in one jurisdiction through settlement while litigating in another), depending on the strength of their position and the willingness of tax authorities to negotiate. Ultimately, the decision reflects a careful weighing of legal, financial, and reputational considerations, with an eye toward maintaining compliance while protecting shareholder value.

Risk Mitigation Practices

Risk mitigation in transfer pricing centers on managing the uncertainty and potential disputes that arise when multinationals allocate profits among related entities across different jurisdictions. Because transfer pricing rules rely on the subjective application of the arm's length principle, companies are vulnerable to challenges from tax authorities, which can lead to adjustments, penalties, and double taxation. Effective risk mitigation practices therefore require a blend of technical compliance, proactive planning, and cooperative engagement with regulators to minimize exposure and provide certainty.

One of the most fundamental practices in mitigating transfer pricing risk is the preparation of detailed documentation. Tax authorities increasingly expect multinationals to maintain comprehensive records that justify their chosen pricing methods, demonstrate compliance with the arm's length principle, and explain the economic rationale for intra-group transactions. Adhering to the OECD's three-tiered documentation standard helps companies present a consistent and transparent picture of their global operations. Such documentation not only reduces the likelihood of adjustments but also provides a strong defense if disputes arise.

Proactive engagement with tax authorities is another cornerstone of risk management. This can take the form of advance pricing agreements, which allow companies to agree in advance on the methodologies used to determine transfer prices. By securing tax authority buy-in before disputes emerge, companies gain greater certainty and reduce the likelihood of future challenges. Similarly, engaging in cooperative compliance programs, where available, builds trust and provides a channel for early dialogue on transfer pricing positions.

Risk mitigation also requires careful design of intra-group transactions and policies. Multinationals must align their transfer pricing arrangements with their actual business operations, ensuring that pricing reflects the functions performed, risks assumed, and assets used by each entity. Artificial or overly aggressive structures are more likely to draw scrutiny, while commercially reasonable and consistent arrangements reduce the perception of tax avoidance. Regular reviews of intercompany pricing policies, particularly in light of changing business models, market conditions, or regulatory environments, help to maintain compliance over time.

Another important practice is the use of benchmarking studies and economic analyses to support pricing decisions. By identifying appropriate comparables and ensuring that margins fall within an acceptable range, companies can demonstrate that their transfer prices are consistent with market conditions. These analyses must be updated periodically, especially when industries undergo rapid change or when a tax authority challenges the reliability of earlier data.

Finally, companies must prepare for the possibility of disputes by considering dispute resolution mechanisms as part of their risk strategy. This includes being familiar with the mutual agreement procedure provided in tax treaties, as well as developing contingency plans for potential litigation or settlement. Having a clear strategy in place enables companies to respond effectively when challenges arise, rather than being caught off guard.

In sum, mitigating transfer pricing risk is not about eliminating disputes altogether, since the inherent subjectivity of the rules makes them unavoidable. Instead, it is about reducing the probability of challenges, strengthening defenses against adjustments, and ensuring that when disputes occur, they can be resolved in a way that minimizes financial and reputational damage. A comprehensive risk mitigation strategy integrates documentation, proactive regulatory engagement, careful policy design, and readiness for resolution, thereby supporting both compliance and the long-term stability of cross-border operations.

Ethical Considerations in Transfer Pricing

Ethical considerations in transfer pricing extend beyond legal compliance and tax minimization, touching on questions of fairness, corporate responsibility, and stakeholder trust. While the arm's-length principle provides a legal framework, the ethical dimension emerges because transfer pricing decisions can shift taxable income between jurisdictions in ways that affect governments, shareholders, employees, and the public at large.

At the heart of the ethical debate is the balance between aggressive tax planning and responsible corporate citizenship. Multinational enterprises often face opportunities to route profits through low-tax jurisdictions by setting intercompany prices that, while technically defensible, may not reflect the true value of local contributions. From a legal standpoint, these arrangements might survive scrutiny if supported by documentation. Yet, from an ethical standpoint, shifting profits away from countries where substantial economic activities take place can deprive those jurisdictions of tax revenues needed for public services. This creates reputational risks for companies that appear to be exploiting loopholes at the expense of society.

Another ethical issue lies in the consistency and transparency of transfer pricing practices. Selectively applying methods that yield the lowest global tax burden, without regard to economic substance, can be perceived as manipulative. Ethical practice requires that companies adopt consistent policies, disclose them transparently, and ensure that they align with the actual creation of value. The OECD's BEPS initiative has heightened expectations around transparency, but compliance with disclosure rules should not be treated as a box-ticking exercise. Ethically, companies should aim to present a fair picture of how profits are allocated and demonstrate that those allocations are justified by real activities and risks.

The treatment of developing countries further amplifies the ethical considerations. Many low-income jurisdictions rely heavily on corporate tax revenues, yet they often lack the resources to challenge complex transfer pricing arrangements. Multinationals may be tempted to take advantage of weaker enforcement environments, shifting profits out of countries that need tax revenue the most. While legally permissible, such actions raise ethical questions about fairness and equity, particularly when companies benefit from infrastructure, labor, and market access in those jurisdictions without contributing proportionately to their tax base.

Finally, transfer pricing decisions must consider the ethical responsibilities to internal stakeholders such as employees and shareholders. Aggressive practices that invite tax audits, prolonged disputes, and large penalties can undermine financial stability and damage long-term value. Ethical governance calls for a balanced approach that minimizes tax risks, protects the company's reputation, and sustains stakeholder confidence. Boards and executives must weigh short-term tax savings against potential long-term costs arising from reputational damage, litigation, or regulatory backlash.

In sum, the ethical dimension of transfer pricing lies in recognizing that decisions about intercompany pricing are not purely technical or legal, but also social. Multinational enterprises must consider the fairness of their tax contributions, the transparency of their practices, and the broader impact on the societies in which they operate.

SAMPLE TRANSFER PRICING CODE OF CONDUCT

Alignment with Value Creation

Transfer pricing policies should ensure that profits are allocated to jurisdictions where substantive economic activities occur and where value is genuinely created. This means respecting the functional contributions of each entity rather than shifting profits to tax havens that lack substance.

Commitment to Transparency

Companies should provide clear, consistent, and accessible explanations of how intercompany pricing is determined. Ethical practice requires going beyond minimum documentation requirements and disclosing, where appropriate, the rationale for profit allocations in ways that demonstrate fairness to stakeholders.

Consistency in Application

Transfer pricing methods should be applied consistently across the organization and over time, unless there are valid business reasons to change. The selective use of methods to maximize tax savings without economic justification undermines both fairness and credibility.

Respect for Local Jurisdictions

Enterprises should acknowledge the fiscal needs of the jurisdictions in which they operate. This includes refraining from exploiting weaker enforcement environments in developing countries or using aggressive structures that erode local tax bases where infrastructure, labor, and markets support business operations.

Risk Prudence and Long-Term Focus

Transfer pricing strategies should avoid excessive risk-taking that could expose the company to large penalties, prolonged disputes, or reputational harm. Ethical governance favors stable, sustainable tax strategies over short-term gains that jeopardize shareholder value and corporate reputation.

Fair Contribution to Society

Companies should view taxes not merely as a cost to be minimized but as a contribution to the societies that enable their success. Ethical transfer pricing supports the principle that corporations, like individuals, have a duty to contribute equitably to the communities and economies from which they benefit.

Accountability and Governance

Boards and senior executives should take responsibility for ensuring that transfer pricing policies reflect not only compliance with the law but also alignment with ethical principles. Regular reviews, internal controls, and clear reporting lines help uphold accountability.

Industry-Specific Issues

Transfer pricing is a particular concern in certain industries that are heavily involved in the creation of intellectual property and intangible assets, as well as the pricing of commodities and the use of marketing hubs. In the following pages, we touch upon the issues faced by several of these industries.

Transfer Pricing in the Technology Sector

The technology sector presents several transfer pricing challenges that are both industry-specific and particularly complex due to the nature of its products and business models. One of the foremost issues is the central role of intangible assets. Technology companies frequently develop intellectual property such as patents, algorithms, and software code, which are highly mobile and difficult to value. Since these intangibles often drive a disproportionate share of profits, allocating returns across jurisdictions becomes contentious. Tax authorities scrutinize arrangements where valuable IP is held in low-tax jurisdictions, raising questions about whether intercompany royalties or cost-sharing agreements reflect arm's length terms.

A related issue is the rapid pace of innovation. Unlike traditional manufacturing, where products may remain stable for years, technology products can become obsolete within months. This short product lifecycle complicates the use of comparables in transfer pricing analyses, as benchmark data quickly loses relevance. Moreover, frequent product iterations blur the lines between development and commercialization, making it challenging to separate routine R&D services from entrepreneurial IP ownership.

Another major complication stems from the digital business models that dominate the sector. Many technology companies generate value from user data, online platforms, or digital services that may not require physical presence in a market. Determining where value is created, and thus where profits should be allocated, is at the heart of international disputes. For example, should advertising revenue from a social media platform be taxed where the platform's servers are located, where the developers reside, or where the users generate content and engagement? These questions lie at the core of OECD's BEPS initiatives and ongoing debates about digital taxation.

Cost sharing arrangements are another focal point. Tech multinationals often establish cost sharing agreements to jointly develop global IP across entities. While these arrangements can be legitimate, disagreements frequently arise over buy-in payments for pre-existing IP and ongoing cost allocations. Valuation disputes often occur because of uncertainty around the future revenue streams tied to a given intangible.

Finally, intercompany services are widespread in the technology sector. Functions such as centralized IT support, cloud infrastructure, engineering services, and platform maintenance must be priced according to the arm's length principle. Distinguishing between low value-adding services that can be allocated on a cost-plus basis versus high-value development services that may warrant a share of residual profits is not always straightforward.

In sum, industry-specific transfer pricing issues in the technology sector revolve around the valuation and allocation of intangible assets, the challenges of rapidly evolving products, the complexities of digital business models, the structuring of cost sharing agreements, and the treatment of intercompany services. These features make the sector one of the most closely monitored by tax authorities worldwide, with frequent audits and disputes over whether reported outcomes align with economic reality.

Transfer Pricing for Pharmaceuticals

The pharmaceuticals sector is among the most complex industries when it comes to transfer pricing, largely due to its dependence on research and development, intellectual property, and heavily regulated supply chains. At the center of transfer pricing issues is the creation, ownership, and exploitation of intangible assets. Drug formulas, patents, and proprietary manufacturing processes are the primary value drivers. Since these intangibles are developed over many years and with substantial investment, allocating the costs and returns across multiple jurisdictions becomes a matter of dispute. Tax authorities are especially concerned when IP is centralized in low-tax jurisdictions while sales and profits are generated worldwide, raising questions about whether arm's length conditions are satisfied.

Another prominent issue is the use of cost sharing and contract R&D arrangements. Multinational pharmaceutical companies often set up structures where subsidiaries contribute to global R&D expenditures in exchange for rights to market the resulting products in specific territories. Disputes frequently arise over the valuation of buy-in payments for pre-existing intangibles and whether ongoing contributions accurately reflect the expected benefits. Similarly, contract R&D subsidiaries may be characterized as routine service providers under cost-plus arrangements, but authorities often challenge whether they in fact bear greater risk and deserve a larger share of returns.

The high-risk nature of drug development also complicates transfer pricing. Most R&D projects fail, while successful drugs can generate enormous profits. Allocating both the costs of unsuccessful projects and the windfall profits from successful ones requires careful economic analysis. Tax authorities may dispute whether the entities funding research truly bore the entrepreneurial risks or whether they were shielded from downside exposure, which would affect how residual profits are shared.

On the commercialization side, the sector faces challenges in intercompany sales of active pharmaceutical ingredients and drugs. Determining the appropriate comparables is difficult because many drugs are unique, protected by patents, and lack direct market benchmarks. In addition, strict regulatory approval requirements restrict substitution, limiting the applicability of standard comparables-based methods. This has led to greater reliance on profit split methods or valuation techniques that model expected cash flows.

Marketing intangibles further complicate matters. In some jurisdictions, tax authorities argue that local distributors create valuable market intangibles through heavy promotional spending and should be entitled to a greater share of profits, rather than being treated as routine limited-risk distributors. The balance between central IP ownership and local market development is often a contentious issue in audits and litigation.

In short, transfer pricing in the pharmaceuticals sector is dominated by disputes over intangible asset valuation, the structuring of R&D and cost-sharing agreements, the treatment of high-risk development cycles, the pricing of intercompany product flows, and the recognition of local marketing intangibles. These industry-specific challenges ensure that the sector remains a major focus of global tax enforcement.

Transfer Pricing for Extractive Industries

Extractive industries (such as mining and oil & gas) present a unique set of transfer pricing challenges, which are shaped by the nature of natural resources, the capital intensity of operations, and the regulatory environments in which they operate. A central issue is the valuation of commodities. Unlike manufactured products, commodities such as crude oil, natural gas, or copper often have publicly quoted market prices. While this seems to simplify pricing, disputes arise when companies sell between affiliates at prices that deviate from published benchmarks. Tax authorities closely scrutinize whether adjustments for quality, delivery terms, transportation, and the timing of sales are appropriate, since small differences can have significant profit-shifting implications.

Intangible assets also complicate transfer pricing in extractive industries. While the resources themselves are physical, significant value arises from proprietary extraction technologies, geological data, and specialized expertise in exploration. Determining whether these intangibles reside in a parent company's headquarters or in local subsidiaries can materially affect profit allocations. Tax authorities increasingly require that the location of functions such as exploration, development, and risk-bearing be aligned with reported profits, rather than attributing outsized returns to holding companies in low-tax jurisdictions.

Another challenge lies in the long investment cycles and high upfront risks characteristic of extractive projects. Exploration and development require enormous capital expenditures over many years before production begins. This raises questions about how to allocate risks and expected returns among group entities. For example, a subsidiary that funds exploration may claim entitlement to entrepreneurial profits if a discovery proves successful, while authorities may argue that other group entities bearing technical or operational risks deserve a share of those returns. The treatment of unsuccessful exploration costs also introduces disputes over whether losses should be retained locally or shared across the group.

Extractive industries are further shaped by resource nationalism and host-country rules. Many governments impose specific pricing formulas, ring-fencing rules, or production-sharing contracts that override arm's length principles. These constraints can create conflicts between satisfying local fiscal regimes and meeting OECD or home-country transfer pricing expectations. For instance, some countries mandate that exports be priced using monthly average market prices, regardless of intragroup contractual terms. Multinationals must navigate these competing obligations while avoiding double taxation.

What is Ring Fencing?

Ring-fencing rules are tax provisions designed to isolate the income and expenses of certain activities (most often extractive industries such as mining and oil & and gas) so that they cannot be combined with income and losses from other business operations of the same taxpayer. The purpose is to prevent companies from using losses or deductions generated in one segment of their operations to reduce taxable profits in another, thereby protecting the host country's tax base that is tied to its natural resources.

In practice, ring-fencing means that each extraction project or license area is treated as a separate fiscal unit for tax purposes. For example, losses from an unprofitable oil field cannot be used to offset profits from a different, more successful field. This ensures that the government receives a fair share of tax revenue from profitable projects, regardless of the overall performance of a multinational. Similarly, capital allowances, exploration costs, and decommissioning expenditures may only be deducted against the income of the project to which they relate.

Marketing hubs present another controversial area. Multinational resource companies often route sales through affiliates in trading centers such as Singapore or Switzerland. These hubs may claim trading margins based on their role in managing logistics, financing, and customer relationships. However, tax authorities in resource-rich countries often argue that these hubs are profit-shifting vehicles and challenge whether they perform sufficient value-adding functions to justify their returns.

Finally, environmental, social, and governance pressures are shaping the sector's transfer pricing issues. Costs related to decommissioning, remediation, and carbon reduction create long-term obligations that must be recognized across group entities. Determining which entity bears these costs and how they affect profitability can influence transfer pricing outcomes, particularly when operations are winding down or transitioning to renewable alternatives.

In sum, industry-specific transfer pricing issues in extractive industries revolve around commodity pricing and comparables, the ownership and location of geological and technical intangibles, the allocation of high-risk exploration and development costs, government-imposed fiscal regimes, the role of marketing hubs, and the treatment of long-term environmental obligations. These factors ensure that transfer pricing in the extractives sector remains contentious and highly sensitive to both global tax standards and host-country interests.

Transfer Pricing for Financial Services

The financial services industry presents some of the most intricate transfer pricing issues because its core business involves capital, risk, and financial instruments; activities that do not fit neatly into the frameworks developed for goods and traditional services. Unlike the manufacturing or distribution sectors, financial institutions deal with highly fungible products, intra-group funding flows, and complex regulatory requirements, which collectively complicate the application of the arm's length principle.

A central issue is the pricing of intra-group financing. Banks and financial groups constantly move capital between affiliates through loans, guarantees, and deposits. Determining an arm's length interest rate requires the consideration of credit ratings, collateral, maturities, and currency risks. The difficulty arises because the subsidiaries of a multinational bank rarely operate as fully independent entities: the parent company's implicit support often lowers borrowing costs, and regulators expect group-level financial strength to backstop local affiliates. Tax authorities stress that intra-group lending must be priced as if the borrower were a standalone entity, but controversies remain over how to quantify the effect of implicit guarantees.

Risk allocation is another defining issue. Financial services companies derive much of their value from their ability to manage credit, market, and liquidity risk. Profits should follow the entity that controls and bears these risks. However, in practice, global banks often centralize risk management in treasury or head-office functions, while profits may be reported in lower-tax jurisdictions. Authorities increasingly scrutinize whether the entities booking profits actually perform decision-making and risk-control activities or merely provide capital.

Regulatory capital requirements further complicate transfer pricing. Banking entities must maintain minimum capital ratios, which can affect how much capital they need to retain in each jurisdiction. Transfer pricing analyses must therefore account not only for the economics of transactions but also for regulatory constraints. For example, thin capitalization rules may overlap with transfer pricing adjustments when assessing intra-group loans.

Intercompany services within banking groups create another layer of complexity. Functions such as IT systems, compliance, legal, and back-office operations are often centralized, but allocating their costs to local affiliates requires careful analysis. Authorities distinguish between routine support services (which may be charged at cost plus a markup) and higher-value functions like portfolio management or structured product design, which could justify a larger profit share.

Another contentious area is financial instruments and derivatives. Banks frequently enter into intra-group derivatives to hedge risks, rebalance portfolios, or transfer exposures between entities. Valuing these transactions at arm's length is challenging given their bespoke nature, illiquid markets, and reliance on internal pricing models. Authorities worry that internal derivatives can be used to shift profits artificially by moving favorable positions into low-tax jurisdictions while leaving unfavorable exposures elsewhere.

Finally, financial services transfer pricing is shaped by the broader regulatory and fiscal environment. Exchange controls, withholding taxes, and restrictions on profit repatriation influence how groups structure intra-group flows. In addition, tax authorities focus heavily on the location of value creation in investment banking, wealth management, and asset management, where cross-border teams contribute to transactions. Allocating profits between origination, execution, and client relationship functions often requires hybrid approaches such as profit splits.

In sum, industry-specific transfer pricing issues for financial services and banking revolve around intra-group financing and guarantees, the allocation of risk and capital, the influence of regulatory capital rules, the treatment of intercompany services, the valuation of complex financial instruments, and the allocation of profits from cross-border client relationships. These issues make the sector one of the most heavily scrutinized by tax authorities, requiring both technical financial expertise and sensitivity to regulatory obligations when designing transfer pricing policies.

Transfer Pricing for Manufacturing and Distribution

The manufacturing and distribution sector faces some of the most established but still challenging transfer pricing issues because its activities involve tangible goods, global supply chains, and varying levels of value-adding functions. Unlike industries centered on intangibles or financial flows, manufacturing and distribution must grapple with how profits are allocated across jurisdictions where physical production, assembly, and sales occur.

For manufacturers, a key issue is the characterization of their role within the multinational group. Some subsidiaries act as full-fledged manufacturers, assuming significant risks and owning valuable intangibles such as process know-how or proprietary production techniques. Others are structured as contract or toll manufacturers, operating under the direction of the parent company with limited risks and assets. The distinction is critical, because it determines whether they are entitled only to a routine cost-plus return or to a share of residual profits. Disputes often arise when tax authorities argue that a supposedly "routine" manufacturer in fact performs entrepreneurial functions and should be compensated accordingly.

Cost allocation and comparables pose another difficulty. Manufacturing often involves high fixed costs, economies of scale, and specialized equipment. Applying traditional transactional methods requires finding suitable independent comparables, but differences in production scale, technology, or capacity utilization can distort results. Adjustments for working capital, market conditions, and capacity usage are often necessary but contentious. Tax authorities closely review whether the losses reported by contract manufacturers or distributors are commercially reasonable, especially if a multinational group as a whole is profitable.

For distribution entities, the primary issue is whether they should be treated as limited-risk distributors or as full-risk entrepreneurs. Limited-risk distributors, who operate under the guidance of the parent company, typically earn a stable but modest return based on the resale price or transactional net margin methods. However, when distributors engage in significant marketing, assume inventory risk, or build local customer relationships, authorities may argue that they are creating "marketing intangibles" and deserve a larger profit share. This is especially relevant in emerging markets where distributors must invest heavily in brand-building and regulatory compliance.

Another issue relates to the intra-group pricing of finished goods. When goods move from a manufacturing affiliate to a distribution affiliate, determining the arm's length transfer price can significantly shift taxable profits between jurisdictions. Price-setting mechanisms must account for differences in markets, distribution channels, and product lifecycles. Authorities often scrutinize whether high-margin goods are consistently routed through low-tax jurisdictions under intercompany contracts.

Business restructurings add complexity. Multinationals frequently reconfigure their supply chains to centralize manufacturing or distribution, sometimes converting full-risk distributors into limited-risk entities. Such restructurings raise questions about exit charges, as tax authorities may contend that local entities transferred valuable intangibles or business opportunities without adequate compensation.

What are Exit Charges?

Exit charges are tax adjustments imposed by a jurisdiction when a business restructuring or reorganization results in the transfer of functions, assets, or risks from a local entity to another group company, which is usually located in a different tax jurisdiction. The rationale is that when a local entity gives up valuable profit-generating capacity (for example, being converted from a full-risk distributor into a limited-risk distributor, or transferring manufacturing know-how to another affiliate), it is effectively transferring economic value out of the jurisdiction. Tax authorities require compensation for this transfer to reflect what an independent third party would have paid under arm's length conditions.

In practice, exit charges are often triggered by supply chain restructurings, the centralization of intangible ownership, or the relocation of manufacturing and distribution functions. For instance, if a multinational consolidates its European distribution network and reduces local affiliates from entrepreneurial distributors to routine service providers, the local entities lose valuable customer relationships, goodwill, or market intangibles. Tax authorities may argue that this constitutes a transfer of business opportunities and demand a one-time exit charge equal to the value of the relinquished assets or functions.

Finally, global events such as trade disputes, supply chain disruptions, or pandemics highlight the importance of aligning transfer pricing policies with economic substance. Manufacturing and distribution affiliates may suffer significant losses due to external shocks, and authorities may challenge whether these losses should be absorbed locally or shared across the group.

In sum, industry-specific transfer pricing issues for manufacturing and distribution revolve around the classification of entities (routine versus entrepreneurial), the availability and adjustment of comparables, the treatment of losses, the recognition of marketing intangibles, the pricing of intercompany sales of goods, and the tax implications of supply chain restructurings. These issues ensure that the sector remains a core focus for transfer pricing enforcement worldwide, particularly given its role in moving tangible value across borders.

Transfer Pricing for E-Commerce

The digital economy sector has become the most debated arena for transfer pricing because of its reliance on intangibles, digital platforms, and data rather than traditional physical assets. Unlike manufacturing or extractive industries, where value creation is tied to tangible activities, digital business models generate significant profits from intellectual property, network effects, and user engagement; elements that are notoriously difficult to price under the arm's length principle.

A central issue is the role of intangible assets. Digital businesses often rely on proprietary algorithms, software platforms, and brand value to generate income. These intangibles are highly mobile and easily centralized in affiliates located in low-tax jurisdictions. Determining an arm's length return for royalties, licensing fees, or cost-sharing arrangements connected to such intangibles is extremely challenging, especially when no comparable third-party transactions exist. Tax authorities therefore focus heavily on whether profits reported in intangible-holding entities are aligned with where the actual functions of development, enhancement, maintenance, protection, and exploitation (DEMPE) take place.

Another defining challenge is the treatment of user participation and data. Social media companies, search engines, and online marketplaces derive substantial value from user-generated content and personal data, yet traditional transfer pricing frameworks struggle to allocate income linked to these contributions. Countries argue that users in their jurisdictions create economic value and should be entitled to a portion of taxable profits.

E-commerce transactions themselves complicate transfer pricing. Online retailers may sell directly to consumers across borders with minimal local infrastructure, often booking revenues through centralized hubs. Authorities question whether limited-risk local subsidiaries (performing marketing, warehousing, or logistics) are appropriately compensated, particularly if they are also engaged in customer acquisition that builds market intangibles. The distinction between routine distribution returns and the entitlement to residual profits from digital brand-building is a frequent audit issue.

Intra-group services also require scrutiny. Digital companies centralize cloud infrastructure, payment systems, IT, and platform development, which are then shared across affiliates. Pricing these services on a cost-plus basis may underestimate their contribution to global profits if they are closely tied to high-value intangibles. Disputes often arise over whether activities such as platform maintenance or digital advertising optimization should be treated as low-value support services or as core entrepreneurial functions.

Finally, the borderless nature of digital commerce means that permanent establishment and nexus rules interact with transfer pricing. A multinational may generate significant revenue in a jurisdiction without having a taxable presence under traditional concepts of "permanent establishment." This gap has led to unilateral measures such as digital services taxes, which increase the risk of double taxation.

What are Digital Services Taxes?

Digital Services Taxes (DSTs) are special taxes introduced by some countries to capture revenue from multinational digital companies that generate significant income within their borders but have little or no physical presence there. Traditional tax rules generally rely on the concept of "permanent establishment," which ties taxing rights to physical presence, but this framework has proven inadequate in the digital economy. DSTs are therefore a unilateral response to the difficulty of taxing highly digitalized business models under existing international rules.

DSTs usually apply to revenues, not profits, that are derived from specific digital activities. Commonly targeted areas include online advertising services, revenues from digital marketplaces that connect sellers and buyers, and fees from the sale of user data. The tax is often levied as a small percentage (commonly 2–7%) of gross revenues linked to users or customers located in the taxing country. For example, France imposes a 3% DST on revenues from digital services earned in its market, while other jurisdictions such as Italy, Spain, and India have enacted similar measures.

In sum, industry-specific transfer pricing issues for the digital economy and e-commerce revolve around the valuation and allocation of intangibles, the recognition of user participation and data as value drivers, the treatment of centralized platforms and digital hubs, the compensation of local affiliates engaged in marketing or customer acquisition, and the broader challenge of aligning taxing rights with value creation in a borderless digital world.

Financial Reporting Issues

Transfer pricing inevitably has an impact on an organization's financial reporting. In the following pages, we note how it interacts with accounting standards, triggers various disclosure requirements, and results in deferred tax issues.

How Transfer Pricing Interacts with Accounting Standards

Transfer pricing sits at the intersection of tax law and financial reporting, and the two regimes pursue different objectives. Transfer pricing aims to allocate taxable income among jurisdictions at arm's length, while IFRS and U.S. GAAP aim to portray the economic results of the consolidated group. Because intercompany prices can be revised through year-end true-ups or tax audits, accountants must translate those tax outcomes into financial-statement effects, often through inventory costing, revenue recognition, impairment testing, income-tax accounting, and related-party disclosures.

A first point of contact is consolidation. Under both IFRS and U.S. GAAP, intercompany profits are eliminated until realized with third parties. If a manufacturing affiliate sells to a distribution affiliate at a markup set for transfer pricing, any unrealized profit embedded in the buyer's closing inventory is eliminated on consolidation. When transfer prices are retroactively "trued up" for tax purposes, groups record adjustments to intercompany revenue/costs and re-compute inventory eliminations; the counterpart is not tax expense by default but the line items originally affected (cost of sales, inventory).

Income-tax accounting then layers on top. A booked or expected transfer pricing adjustment can create current tax and deferred tax consequences. If a true-up changes the local tax base of inventory or other assets without changing the consolidated carrying amount, then temporary differences arise and deferred taxes are recognized in the seller's or buyer's jurisdiction, with tax expense in the income statement unless the underlying item went to other comprehensive income or equity.

Intangibles are another pressure point. A transfer of IP between affiliates for tax purposes at an arm's-length price does not create consolidated profit, but it can change local carrying amounts and tax bases, thereby producing deferred taxes. Subsequent impairment testing uses consolidated cash flows independent of tax transfer prices, though local books may show different amortization patterns and tax shields.

Business combinations and restructurings create distinct tensions. Many tax-motivated supply-chain restructurings trigger exit charges for transfer pricing; in financial reporting, internal transfers within the group are eliminated. Nevertheless, exit charges recognized in local statutory accounts affect current and deferred taxes in consolidation, and can prompt impairment testing if they signal reduced future cash flows for local cash generating units.

Transfer Pricing Disclosure Requirements

Under GAAP, transfer pricing touches multiple disclosure areas because intercompany arrangements affect how results are measured internally, how taxes are recognized, and how related-party dealings are explained to readers. Although profits on intercompany sales are eliminated on consolidation, the policies, exposures, and consequences of transfer pricing decisions must still be described where material. The core disclosure areas are related-party disclosures, segment reporting, income tax disclosures (including uncertain tax positions), and, where relevant, inventory, revenue, contingencies, and financial instruments.

Related-party disclosures require an entity to describe the nature of its relationships and the substance of significant transactions with affiliates. For transfer pricing, that typically means explaining material intercompany arrangements such as royalties, cost-sharing or development agreements, service charges, intercompany sales of goods, shared logistics or IT, and funding or guarantees. U.S. GAAP mandates the disclosure of the dollar amounts of transactions and outstanding balances, terms and settlement policies, and how prices were determined (for example, whether charges are based on cost-plus, resale-minus, negotiated rates, or other internal formulas). If pricing policies or the structure of intragroup arrangements change in ways that materially affect comparability between periods, then those changes and their effects on the financial statements should be described.

Segment reporting can bring transfer prices to the foreground because internal measures provided to the chief operating decision maker may reflect intersegment transfer prices. When such prices materially influence reported segment revenue or profit, U.S. GAAP requires the disclosure of the basis of intersegment pricing and reconciliations from segment measures to consolidated totals. If a change in transfer pricing systematically shifts profitability among segments, the disclosure should clarify the basis and magnitude so that trend analysis is not misleading.

Income tax disclosures are often the most consequential area for transfer pricing. U.S. GAAP requires a reconciliation of the reported effective tax rate to the statutory rate; transfer pricing effects commonly appear in this reconciliation through foreign rate differentials, prior-period adjustments, audit settlements, or discrete true-ups. Entities must also present the significant components of deferred tax assets and liabilities and any valuation allowance; transfer pricing can influence these amounts through intercompany profit eliminations, local-book versus tax-basis differences arising from intragroup IP transfers, and year-end pricing adjustments that alter the tax basis of inventory or other assets without changing their consolidated carrying amount. Uncertain tax positions tied to transfer pricing are subject to the recognition and measurement guidance for tax uncertainties; required disclosures include a tabular rollforward of unrecognized tax benefits, the total amount that would affect the effective tax rate if recognized, the entity's policy for interest and penalties and the amounts recognized, the years open to examination by major jurisdiction, and a narrative about matters reasonably possible to change in the next twelve months (for example, an anticipated resolution of a transfer pricing audit or advance pricing agreement).

Because transfer pricing true-ups often flow through cost of sales or operating expenses rather than tax expense, accounting policy disclosures should make clear how such adjustments are classified and when they are recognized. If pricing affects inventory, for instance, through intercompany markups that are eliminated until sales to third parties, entities should explain the inventory costing policy and, when material, the impact of elimination entries and any lower-of-cost-and-net-realizable-value assessments that incorporate those effects. For intercompany services or bundled arrangements that also affect revenue recognition to external customers, the revenue policy note should remain consistent with the pattern of transfer of control; while intercompany revenue is eliminated, the narrative should avoid implying that tax transfer prices drive recognition to third parties.

Transfer pricing can also surface in other notes. If intragroup financing is significant, the financial instruments and guarantees footnotes may need to discuss intercompany loans, stated rates, whether terms are off-market, expected credit losses on those balances, and any guarantees or support arrangements that could affect measurement. If a supply-chain restructuring gives rise to local statutory exit charges or to disputes that are not income-tax uncertainties (for example, customs or indirect-tax matters), the contingencies note should describe the nature of the exposure and, where estimable, the possible loss or range of loss. Interim reporting requires timely disclosure of material discrete tax items and significant changes in unrecognized tax benefits arising from transfer pricing events during the quarter.

In practice, robust U.S. GAAP compliance means knitting these threads into a coherent story: describing related-party pricing frameworks and any significant changes; explaining how internal transfer prices influence segment results and the basis for those prices; providing clear tax disclosures that isolate transfer pricing effects in the rate reconciliation, deferred taxes, and uncertain tax positions. Done well, the disclosures allow readers to understand the economic substance of intragroup arrangements.

Deferred Tax Implications of Transfer Pricing

Transfer pricing arrangements can create significant deferred tax implications because the income recognized for financial reporting purposes often differs from the taxable income recognized in each jurisdiction. These differences typically arise when tax authorities adjust intercompany transfer prices to align with the arm's-length principle, while consolidated financial statements may already reflect different allocations of revenue and expense.

Deferred tax assets and liabilities arise from temporary differences between the carrying amount of assets and liabilities in consolidated financial statements and their corresponding tax bases in individual jurisdictions. For example, if a tax authority requires higher transfer prices for goods sold into its jurisdiction, the local subsidiary may recognize higher taxable income than what is recorded in the group's financial statements. This creates a taxable temporary difference and, therefore, a deferred tax liability. Conversely, the selling entity may recognize a lower taxable profit than reported in the consolidated financials, leading to deductible temporary differences and deferred tax assets.

The deferred tax effect is recognized when the intercompany transaction impacts the profit or loss of the consolidated group but has not yet resulted in a tax consequence at the entity level. For instance, intercompany sales of inventory or fixed assets often create mismatches because profits are eliminated on consolidation but remain recognized for tax purposes until the goods are sold externally. This requires recording deferred taxes on unrealized intercompany profits.

Because transfer pricing is frequently scrutinized by tax authorities, companies may face uncertain tax positions regarding the acceptability of their intercompany pricing. Deferred tax accounting under ASC 740 or IAS 12 requires companies to evaluate whether deferred tax assets can be realized and whether reserves are needed for uncertain tax positions. If future taxable income is unlikely to absorb deferred tax assets arising from transfer pricing adjustments, a valuation allowance must be established.

The OECD's BEPS framework has increased the likelihood of transfer pricing adjustments across multiple jurisdictions. Companies must maintain sufficient documentation to support their intercompany pricing, not only to defend against additional tax assessments but also to properly calculate deferred tax positions under local accounting rules.

In summary, the deferred tax implications of transfer pricing stem from timing differences between financial reporting and tax recognition of intercompany transactions, the elimination of unrealized profits in consolidation, and the uncertainties created by potential transfer pricing disputes. These effects require careful monitoring and documentation to ensure compliance and accurate financial reporting.

EXAMPLE

A multinational corporation, Underwood Inc., operates through a parent company based in the United States and several subsidiaries around the world. One of its key subsidiaries, located in Singapore, manufactures specialized electronic components that are sold both to third-party customers and to another subsidiary in Germany that integrates the components into finished products. The internal transfer price set between the Singapore and German subsidiaries has a direct impact on how profits are reported across the group and ultimately on the consolidated financial statements.

Initially, the transfer price for the components was established at $1,000 per unit. The Singapore entity produced the goods at a cost of $600 per unit, realizing a $400 profit per unit. The German subsidiary purchased the units at this price, included them in inventory, and eventually sold the finished goods to external customers at a higher price. For local statutory purposes, Singapore recognized $400 of profit per unit, subject to its local tax rate, while Germany would only recognize profit once external sales occurred. In the consolidated financial statements, however, the $1,000 intercompany sale and the $1,000 purchase were eliminated, leaving only the external revenue and cost structure visible. The consolidated group reflected an economic profit equal to the total margin from third-party sales, not the split created by transfer pricing between entities.

The financial statement complications emerged when the German tax authority challenged the transfer price. It argued that the $1,000 price overstated the value of the components and that an arm's-length price should have been $800 per unit. This adjustment meant that, for tax purposes, the German subsidiary's deductible costs were reduced and its taxable profits increased, resulting in an additional tax liability. For Underwood's consolidated financial statements, the adjustment triggered several effects. First, a deferred tax liability was recognized to reflect the likelihood of an additional tax payment in Germany. At the same time, the U.S. parent company, which ultimately owned the Singapore operations, anticipated a reduced taxable base in its home jurisdiction, creating a deferred tax asset. The net impact of these positions slightly increased the group's overall effective tax rate, even though the consolidated pretax profit remained unchanged after eliminations.

Moreover, the adjustment had implications for inventory valuation. At the point of consolidation, the German subsidiary's inventory carried an embedded intercompany markup of $400 per unit. When the goods were still unsold at year-end, the consolidated financial statements required elimination of that unrealized profit, reducing inventory and consolidated earnings. With the tax authority's adjustment lowering the markup to $200, the elimination entries also changed, thereby altering the balance sheet valuation of inventory and the associated deferred tax entries.

The case of Underwood Inc. demonstrates that while transfer pricing may be a compliance exercise at the local entity level, its financial reporting effects are broad. Consolidated financial statements must carefully eliminate intercompany transactions to avoid overstating revenue, adjust for deferred taxes created by mismatches between accounting and tax bases, and disclose uncertain tax positions arising from ongoing disputes. The economic outcome of the group does not change, but the allocation of profits, the recognition of tax liabilities, and the transparency of disclosures are all shaped by transfer pricing policies and the scrutiny of tax authorities.

The Role of Technology in Transfer Pricing Compliance

Technology now plays a central role in helping multinationals manage transfer pricing compliance, as the scale, complexity, and scrutiny of intercompany transactions have increased dramatically. Historically, transfer pricing documentation was prepared in spreadsheets and maintained in disparate files across jurisdictions, creating a high risk of inconsistency and incomplete information. Today, specialized transfer pricing software, integrated enterprise resource planning systems, and advanced analytics are transforming how companies approach compliance.

One of the most important contributions of technology is the ability to centralize and automate data collection. Transfer pricing documentation requires detailed information on intercompany transactions, functional analyses, and financial results across multiple subsidiaries. The manual compilation of this data is error-prone and time consuming, particularly when subsidiaries use different accounting systems. Modern platforms can extract transactional data directly from ERP systems such as SAP or Oracle, consolidate it, and align it with transfer pricing policies. This not only ensures consistency in reporting but also reduces the administrative burden of assembling local files and country-by-country reports under OECD guidelines.

Technology also supports compliance through real-time monitoring and analytics. Advanced tools can flag unusual intercompany margins, deviations from policy benchmarks, or inconsistent allocations of service costs before they become material compliance risks. Predictive analytics and artificial intelligence can be used to model arm's-length ranges and evaluate whether current pricing practices fall within acceptable thresholds. By identifying risks early, companies can take corrective actions rather than waiting for tax authorities to raise challenges during audits.

Document management is another critical area where technology enhances compliance. Regulatory frameworks increasingly demand contemporaneous documentation that demonstrates adherence to the arm's-length principle. Digital platforms can create a standardized repository of master files, local files, and country-by-country reports, ensuring that updates are synchronized across jurisdictions. Version control features allow companies to track changes, manage approvals, and demonstrate to regulators that documentation is current and properly maintained.

Finally, technology strengthens a multinational's transparency and defense strategies in the event of a tax audit. Transfer pricing software can generate automated audit trails that show how intercompany prices were set, which data sources were used, and how comparables were selected. This level of detail gives companies greater confidence in defending their positions and reduces the perception of arbitrary or unsupported pricing methods. It also facilitates better communication with external advisors and tax authorities, as standardized outputs can be shared more easily than ad hoc spreadsheets.

In sum, the role of technology in transfer pricing compliance is not limited to efficiency gains; it fundamentally reshapes the compliance process. By centralizing data, enabling real-time monitoring, enhancing documentation management, and improving audit readiness, technology allows multinationals to manage transfer pricing risks more proactively. This is increasingly vital in a regulatory environment characterized by heightened scrutiny and cross-border information sharing.

EXAMPLE

A global pharmaceutical company, Albatross Group, operates research centers in the United States, manufacturing plants in Ireland, and distribution subsidiaries across Europe and Asia. Because of the high volume of intercompany royalties, service charges, and product flows, transfer pricing compliance has historically been a major challenge. In the past, each subsidiary generated its own spreadsheets to document intercompany charges, and the headquarters tax team struggled to reconcile figures across dozens of local files. Errors in data mapping led to inconsistencies, and local tax audits frequently uncovered documentation gaps.

To address this, Albatross implemented a transfer pricing compliance platform that connects directly to its enterprise resource planning system. The tool extracts intercompany transaction data daily, categorizes it according to predefined transfer pricing policies, and applies benchmarked profit margins automatically. For example, when the U.S. entity licenses intellectual property to the Irish manufacturer, the system calculates the royalty charge using a fixed formula and posts the entry simultaneously to both entities' ledgers. This eliminates mismatches that previously arose when subsidiaries calculated charges independently.

The ERP integration also allows for real-time monitoring of margins. When the Irish manufacturing subsidiary ships products to the German distributor, the system compares the resulting gross margin in Germany to the benchmark range established in the transfer pricing documentation. If the margin falls outside the expected range, the tool flags the transaction for review and adjustment before the quarter-end close. This feature prevents the company from reporting results that could later trigger transfer pricing disputes.

In terms of documentation, the platform automatically generates master files, local files, and country-by-country reports using standardized templates that align with OECD and local requirements. When tax authorities in France request evidence of the arm's-length nature of service charges, Albatross can provide a digital local file within days, complete with benchmarking studies and transaction details sourced directly from the ERP. Because all files are stored in a central repository with audit trails, management can show regulators exactly when and how documents were updated.

The technology also enhances Albatross' ability to respond to tax audits. In a recent German audit, the authorities questioned the royalty rate applied by the U.S. parent to the Irish subsidiary. The compliance platform produced a detailed report showing the underlying comparables, the policy logic embedded in the ERP, and the approval history of the royalty agreement. This transparency helped the company defend its position and shortened the audit process.

Landmark Transfer Pricing Cases

Certain transfer pricing cases are especially well-known, and their outcomes have had a significant influence on how governments have chosen to deal with transfer pricing methodologies. The key cases are as follows:

- *GlaxoSmithKline (U.S., 2006).* The Glaxo case was one of the first major global transfer pricing disputes to spotlight the allocation of profits from marketing intangibles. The IRS argued that Glaxo shifted profits abroad by overstating the value of marketing activities in foreign subsidiaries while undervaluing the role of U.S.-developed patents and formulas. The $3.4 billion settlement underscored the difficulty of distinguishing between the value of trademarks, patents, and marketing intangibles. This case informed later OECD BEPS guidance, which emphasized aligning profit allocation with the actual development, enhancement, maintenance, protection, and exploitation (DEMPE) functions of intangibles. Regulators worldwide began scrutinizing whether affiliates truly performed the functions and bore the risks that justified their share of intangible returns.

- *Coca-Cola (U.S., 2020).* The Coca-Cola case reinforced the importance of consistent application of transfer pricing methodologies over time. Coca-Cola had long allocated substantial profits to foreign bottlers under an agreement with the IRS, but the agency later argued that this approach no longer reflected arm's-length outcomes given the enormous value of U.S.-owned intangibles like trademarks and formulas. The U.S. Tax Court largely sided with the IRS, imposing adjustments exceeding $9 billion. This case highlighted that even long-standing agreements can be revisited if they deviate from the arm's-length principle. For OECD BEPS, it underscored the need for contemporaneous documentation and the ongoing review of intercompany arrangements, especially when intangibles drive profitability.

- *Nestlé (Brazil, 1997).* Nestlé's dispute with the Brazilian authorities centered on the export pricing of coffee. Brazil has historically applied fixed-margin formulas rather than traditional OECD arm's-length methods, and the courts sided with the tax authority in rejecting Nestlé's intercompany pricing. This case demonstrated how local deviations from OECD standards can create compliance risks. It also showed the importance of adapting transfer pricing policies to jurisdiction-specific rules rather than relying solely on OECD frameworks. In the BEPS context, Nestlé's case highlighted the global diversity of transfer pricing regimes and fueled discussions about simplifying compliance while respecting local sovereignty in tax administration.

- *Medtronic (U.S., 2016–2022).* The Medtronic litigation revolved around the difficulty of valuing unique intangibles. The IRS contended that Medtronic's licensing arrangements undervalued U.S. technology transferred to its Puerto Rican affiliate, while the company argued that its comparable uncontrolled transaction analysis was appropriate. The courts initially supported Medtronic, but appeals and remands showed how subjective valuations can be.

This case influenced OECD BEPS by reinforcing the limitations of rigidly applying the comparable uncontrolled transaction method to unique intangibles and by pushing regulators toward broader acceptance of profit split methods where no close comparables exist. It emphasized that intangible-heavy industries, such as pharmaceuticals and medical devices, require nuanced approaches that are aligned with value creation.

- *DHL (Germany, 1997).* The DHL case involved the allocation of profits to a Bermuda subsidiary that legally owned trademarks but lacked substance in terms of personnel and operational functions. German authorities successfully argued that Bermuda's entitlement to profits was disproportionate to the functions and risks actually assumed. The case became a classic illustration of the principle that profit allocation must follow economic substance rather than legal form. OECD BEPS incorporated this lesson directly into Actions 8–10, which require that profits from intangibles be aligned with the entity performing DEMPE functions. The DHL decision anticipated BEPS's central theme: preventing the use of low-substance entities to shift profits into tax havens.

Taken together, these cases illustrate the evolution of transfer pricing enforcement from focusing narrowly on transactional comparables to a broader emphasis on value creation and economic substance. Glaxo and Coca-Cola highlighted disputes over marketing and trade intangibles, leading to BEPS reforms that require clear evidence of DEMPE functions. Nestlé showed the risks of divergent local rules, prompting the OECD to push for consistency while recognizing national discretion. Medtronic highlighted the practical challenges of valuing unique intangibles and supported the shift toward profit-split methods in complex industries. DHL underscored the need for substance in ownership structures, a principle that now underpins anti-avoidance measures worldwide.

The cumulative influence of these cases is visible in OECD BEPS guidance, which harmonized global rules by requiring profit alignment with real activities, improved transparency through country-by-country reporting, and enhanced documentation standards. Multinationals now face stricter requirements to demonstrate that intercompany arrangements are not only legally structured but also economically justified by actual functions, assets, and risks.

Summary

Transfer pricing is a central pillar of international taxation, designed to ensure that cross-border transactions within multinationals are conducted at arm's length. This course traced its evolution from early U.S. safeguards in the 1920s to today's global framework anchored in OECD and UN guidance. The material explained how the arm's length principle underpins nearly all regulatory approaches, while also highlighting the challenges of applying it in industries dominated by intangibles, digital platforms, and complex supply chains. Key methods, including CUP, resale price, cost-plus, TNMM, and profit split, were discussed alongside criteria for selecting the most appropriate approach. Throughout, emphasis was placed on the role of functional analysis, comparability adjustments, and benchmarking studies in aligning intercompany transactions with market-based outcomes.

Beyond methods, the course addressed compliance, risk management, and dispute resolution. It reviewed OECD's three-tiered documentation framework, country-specific variations, and common pitfalls that invite scrutiny. Practical strategies such as advance pricing agreements, mutual agreement procedures, and ethical considerations were examined in the context of minimizing disputes and maintaining fairness. Industry-specific issues, including those affecting technology, pharmaceuticals, extractive industries, and e-commerce, were also explored, demonstrating how transfer pricing intersects with financial reporting, deferred taxes, and evolving global reforms. Taken together, the course prepares practitioners to manage transfer pricing in a way that balances regulatory compliance, corporate strategy, and the shifting international tax landscape.

Glossary

A

Advance pricing agreement. A formal arrangement between a multinational and one or more tax authorities that establish, in advance of actual transactions, an agreed-upon method for determining transfer prices.

Arm's length transaction. A transaction in which related parties set prices and terms as if they were independent entities acting in their own best economic interests under comparable market conditions.

B

Base Erosion and Profit Shifting Project. An initiative led by OECD and the G20 to address tax avoidance strategies used by multinational enterprises.

Benchmarking study. A systematic process of identifying and analyzing comparable companies or transactions to establish an arm's length range of results.

C

Comparable uncontrolled price method. A transfer pricing method that determines the arm's length price of a controlled transaction by comparing it to the price charged in a comparable transaction between independent enterprises under similar circumstances.

Cost-plus method. A pricing approach where the transfer price is determined by adding an appropriate mark-up to the supplier's production costs to reflect an arm's length profit.

D

Digital services tax. A special tax introduced by some countries to capture revenue from multinational digital companies that generate significant income within their borders but have little or no physical presence there.

Double taxation. When two countries seek to tax the same income.

E

Exit charges. Tax adjustments imposed by a jurisdiction when a business restructuring or reorganization results in the transfer of functions, assets, or risks from a local entity to another group company, which is usually located in a different tax jurisdiction.

External comparables. Transactions between independent, unrelated parties that are used as benchmarks to test whether the pricing of controlled transactions between related entities is consistent with the arm's length principle.

I

Internal comparables. Transactions conducted between a taxpayer and an independent third party that are used as benchmarks to evaluate the arm's length nature of the taxpayer's related-party transactions.

M

Mutual agreement procedure. Dispute resolution mechanisms provided under bilateral tax treaties to address issues of double taxation and inconsistent tax treatment, particularly in the context of transfer pricing.

P

Profit split method. A method that allocates the combined profits (or losses) of related entities from controlled transactions based on the relative value of each party's contributions to those transactions.

R

Resale price method. A method of determining an arm's length price by starting with the resale price at which a product is sold to an independent customer and subtracting an appropriate gross margin to cover the reseller's functions, risks, and assets.

Ring fencing. Tax provisions designed to isolate the income and expenses of certain activities, so that they cannot be combined with income and losses from other business operations of the same taxpayer.

T

Transactional net margin method. A method that evaluates whether the profits earned by a taxpayer in controlled transactions are consistent with the arm's length principle by comparing the net profit margin relative to an appropriate base (such as costs, sales, or assets) against those earned by independent entities in comparable circumstances.

Transfer pricing. The pricing of goods, services, or intangible assets exchanged between the related entities of a multinational enterprise.

Index

www.ingramcontent.com/pod-product-compliance
Lightning Source LLC
Chambersburg PA
CBHW051420200326
41520CB00023B/7314